TRAD JAZZ
for
TENOR BANJO

BY
Dick Sheridan

Spanning Over 100 Years
From the Jazz Age to the Present

Featuring 35 of the
Best Known Traditional Favorites

Dixieland Standards in Standard Keys
Melodies in Notation & Tablature
Chord Symbols & Diagrams
CD Recording
Lyrics
Background Information & Commentaries

Design & Typography by Roy "Rick" Dains

ISBN 978-1-57424-311-6

Copyright ©2014 CENTERSTREAM Publishing, LLC
P. O. Box 17878 - Anaheim Hills, CA 92817
email: centerstream@aol.com • web: centerstream-usa.com

DEDICATION

EMANUEL "MANNY" SAYLES
1907–1986
PRESERVATION HALL, NEW ORLEANS, 1984
Photo by Permission: Shirley Woodcock-Kolb

TABLE OF CONTENTS

CD LISTING

To enhance your enjoyment of this book, a recording of each song is included on the accompanying CD. Solo piano accompaniment is sythesized from the computer notation software. You'll find this especially helpful if you're unfamiliar with a particular piece. Songs are clearly presented to allow you to play along with either the melody or the chords at the suggested tempo, or simply to enjoy listening to the song. Songs are placed on the CD in the same order as they appear in the book.

INTRODUCTION

"Ashes to ashes, dust to dust,
if my blues don't get you my jazzin' must ..."
- St. Louis Blues

Trad Jazz and the banjo. Like ham and eggs, pepper and salt, black and white, one goes with the other. We'd be less for the loss if there were a separation.

By any other name, Trad Jazz is just that: traditional jazz. Some call it Dixieland, New Orleans jazz, classic or early jazz. It's all the same. How and when the name gained popularity is somewhat obscure, just as is the origin of the word "jazz". It may have gained usage in Europe, a more universal name than Dixieland which was losing favor in some quarters because of its association with troublesome issues of the early South.

Whatever name we choose to call it, it refers to that style of music developed initially in New Orleans in the early 1900s. From there it soon took root in Memphis, Kansas City, Chicago, New York, and thence around the world. An outgrowth of ragtime, primitive and unsophisticated, it was performed mostly by unschooled musicians playing by ear and relying on familiar ragtime numbers, marches, spirituals, classical strains, and popular tunes of the day. The legacy of this music continues to the present, augmented by newer material along the way, but still strongly reflecting the popular songs of the early 1900s, the roaring 20s, and into the 30s.

Who were the early musicians and bands that made these tunes popular? It's a long list but one that certainly includes Buddy Bolden, Bunk Johnson, Kid Ory, Sidney Bechet, George Lewis, Jelly Roll Morton, Red Allen, Louis Armstrong, and bands like the Original Dixieland Jazz Band, the New Orleans Rhythm Kings, King Oliver's Creole Band, and Morton's Red Hot Peppers.

It was about the start of the 1900s that the tango was all the rage and the banjo was a vital part of its popularity. This gave rise to the term "tango banjo" which allegedly evolved into the name "tenor banjo". Even though public taste drifted away from the tango and ragtime, the banjo remained popular and soon became an essential band instrument with the emerging new style of jazz.

Not all of these banjos were tenors. Some were plectrums, others in guitar tuning. Some were hybrids like the combination guitar-banjo with a guitar neck and a banjo head. But a band without a banjo ~ no matter what its tuning or configuration - would seem lackluster, bland, and uninspiring.

It should be noted that today plectrum tuning of the banjo (CGBD) is preferred by some, and less so the guitar tuned banjo (DGBE). With both of these tunings the smaller interval between upper strings permits easier single-note melody playing, but from some perspectives the "punch" of tenor chording seems replaced by a mellow sound more suited to contemporary music than historic jazz.

Like a viola, the tenor banjo is tuned in fifths - CGDA. Listening to recordings of early bands you can hear its sound soar above the brass and reeds. It added percussion along with chordal harmony when there wasn't a piano. Being lightweight and portable, it proved ideal for street parades and marches to the cemetery.

Initially the banjo was played rather simply keeping 4/4 time by accenting the 2nd and 4th beat or keeping a straight steady four strums to the measure. This style can be heard in the playing of early banjoists like Lawrence Marrero, Emanuel Sayles, and Johnny St. Cyr (who was part of Louis Armstrong's "Hot Five" and "Hot Seven") and Jelly Roll Morton's 1930's Chicago-based "Red Hot Peppers."

Although there are exceptions, generally soloing didn't come until later, inspired by the virtuosic talent of such players as Eddy Peabody and Harry Reser. But even today with current revival bands, the "pure and simple" but powerful accompaniment style is preferred by many to flamboyant razzle-dazzle, what folk banjoist Pete Seeger referred to as "pyrotechnical."

It must be said that many banjoists also played guitar and that guitars were often a part of early bands and their later revivals. Eddie Condon, a product of the 1930's Chicago school of Dixieland, was a well-known guitarist and trad band leader who started by playing the tenor banjo, then switched to plectrum tuning on a tenor guitar, and finally to a plectrum guitar. Condon moved to NYC and ran successful jazz clubs for 20 years. One venue was in Greenwich Village, and during its time there a retired policeman I met several years ago told me how he would follow Eddie home late at night after the club closed. Eddie would be carrying the evening's take and the policeman followed slowly at a distance in his patrol car just to be sure Eddie got home safely. I was also told that model trains were set up in the club's basement providing an escape for Eddie and the musicians from the crowds and glad-handers.

Author Dick Sheridan, banjo, and his Syracuse, NY based Soda Ash Six Dixieland Jazz Band, circa 1970s.

The banjo remains as popular today as it did in early years and is very much in evidence with contemporary trad bands. A short sampling of current festival bands – the New Black Eagles, High Sierra, Grand Dominion, along with international inputs from Europe, Asia, and elsewhere – find the banjo well ensconced. And indeed this was certainly true for preceding revival groups like the Dukes Of Dixieland, Turk Murphy's Jazz Band, Lu Watters Yerba Buena Jazz Band, and the iconic Firehouse Five Plus Two.

Admittedly, banjo playing tends to be a male dominated field, but there are notable exceptions going back to the turn of the 20th Century, on to vaudeville, and continuing right up to the present day. Among the current forefront are Cynthia Sayer who plays with Woody Allen's New Orleans Jazz Band, Cathy Reilly (wife of Fred "Mickey" Finn), Katie Cavera, and Amy Sharpe – all wonderful virtuosi, and all 4-string players both tenor and plectrum.

And there are many other lady banjoists including Joan Dragon, a former student, who went on to play with the celebrated chain of banjo parlors called Your Father's Mustache. Joan has been active in promoting Dixieland events and is the past director of the Suncoast Jazz Festival in Clearwater, Florida.

The following collection contains some of the best trad jazz songs being played around the world. You're bound to hear one or more of them wherever a traditional jazz band is playing. If you're a newcomer to the idiom, you'll find standards that will soon be numbered among your favorites. For the experienced trad banjoist here's an opportunity to review accurate melodies and chords as well as a chance to learn some new tunes while refining some of those already known. Even if you don't play the banjo, these songs may well be the inspiration to take up the instrument and join the swelling ranks of those who have found the banjo fun, challenging, and immensely rewarding – especially when playing the legendary style inspired by the jazz of old New Orleans.

JUST A CLOSER WALK WITH THEE

Tenor Banjo tuning: CGDA

TRADITIONAL

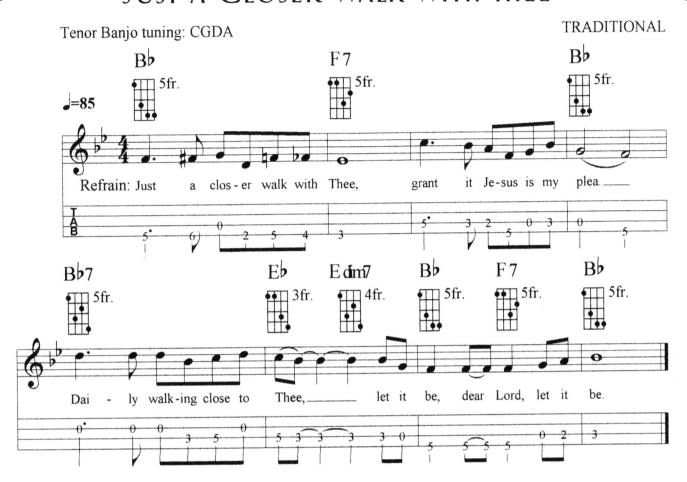

Verse 1: I am weak but Thou art strong;
Jesus, keep me from all wrong;
I'll be satisfied as long as I
Walk, let me walk, close to Thee.
(Refrain)

Verse 2: When my feeble life is o'er,
Time for me will be no more;
Guide me gently, safely o'er
To Thy kingdon shore, to Thy shore.
(Refrain)

The story is told about two older ladies with limited vision who were sitting in the audience of a vaudeville palace where each upcoming act was announced with a placard set out on an easel. One lady turned to the other and asked her if she would read the chart and tell her what the upcoming act would be. With sight not much better than her friend, she looked, squinted, and said, "It's the refrain... the refrain from "Spitting."

AFTER YOU'VE GONE
(1918)
Tenor Banjo tuning: CGDA

HENRY CREAMER

JOHN T. LAYTON

AFTER YOU'VE GONE

Most songs start with a tonic or dominant 7th chord, but here we have an exception, since a subdominant chord begins the progression. Typically, jazz bands play the song through once slowly then double-time and kick it into high gear. The last two measures are often cut, two measures added, and the next solo instrument fills them in as a pick-up.

Some day, when you grow lone - ly, your heart will break like mine and

you'll want me on - ly.___ Af - ter you've gone, af - ter you've gone a - way.___

The Original Moonlight Serenaders
Circa 1920

A Good Man is Hard to Find
(1918)

Tenor Banjo tuning: CGDA

EDDIE GREEN

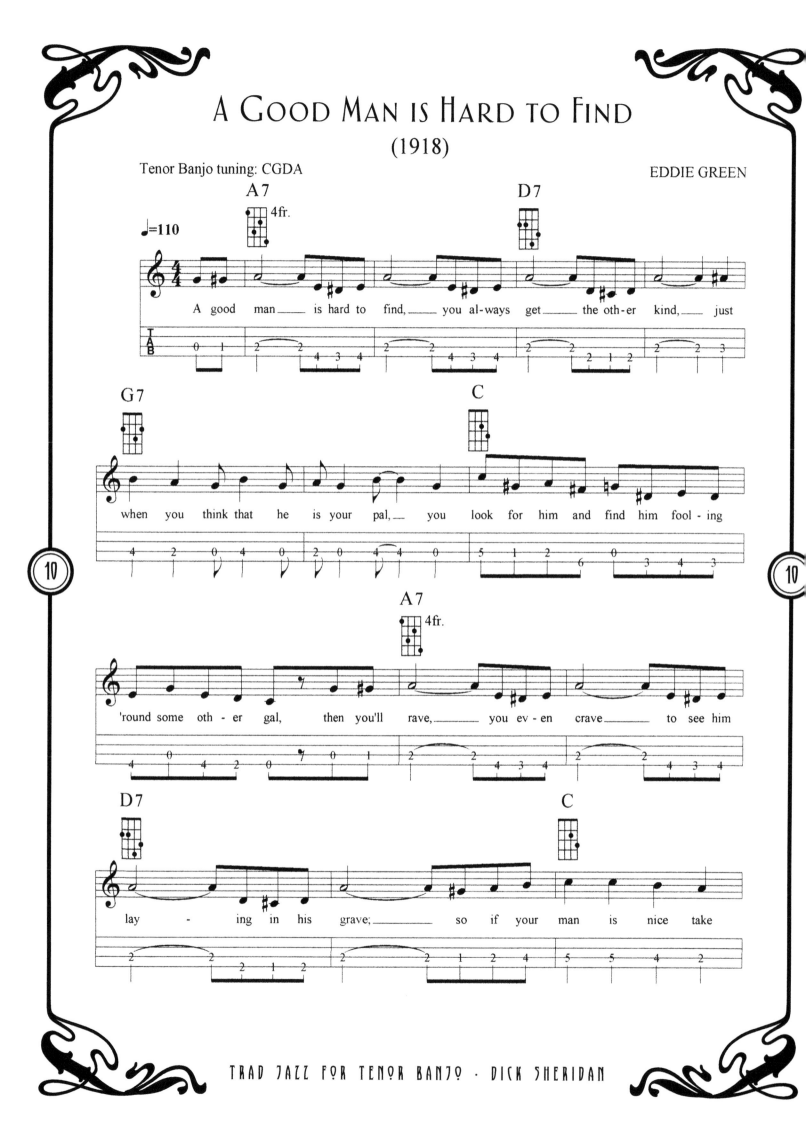

A Good Man is Hard to Find

Few songbirds can belt out this song like Pat Yankee, one of the most popular West Coast trad jazz vocalists. When she sings it, you know she means it. So take heed, ladies, and follow Pat's advice: there may be some real wisdom contained in these lyrics.

my ad - vice and hug him in the morn - ing, kiss him ev - 'ry night, give him plen - ty lov - in'

treat him right, for a good man now a - days is hard to find. _____

CHINATOWN, MY CHINATOWN

(1910)
Tenor Banjo tuning: CGDA

WILLIAM JEROME

JEAN SCHWARTZ

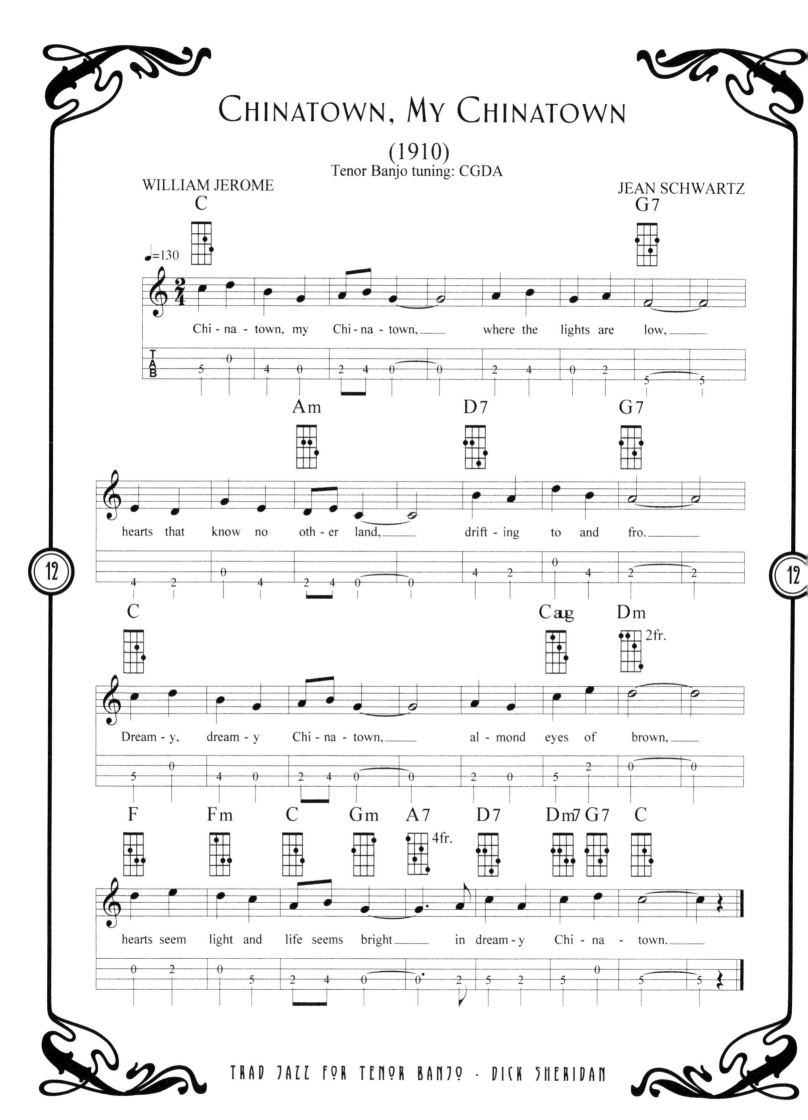

ALEXANDER'S RAGTIME BAND
(1911)

Tenor banjo tuning: CGDA

IRVING BERLIN

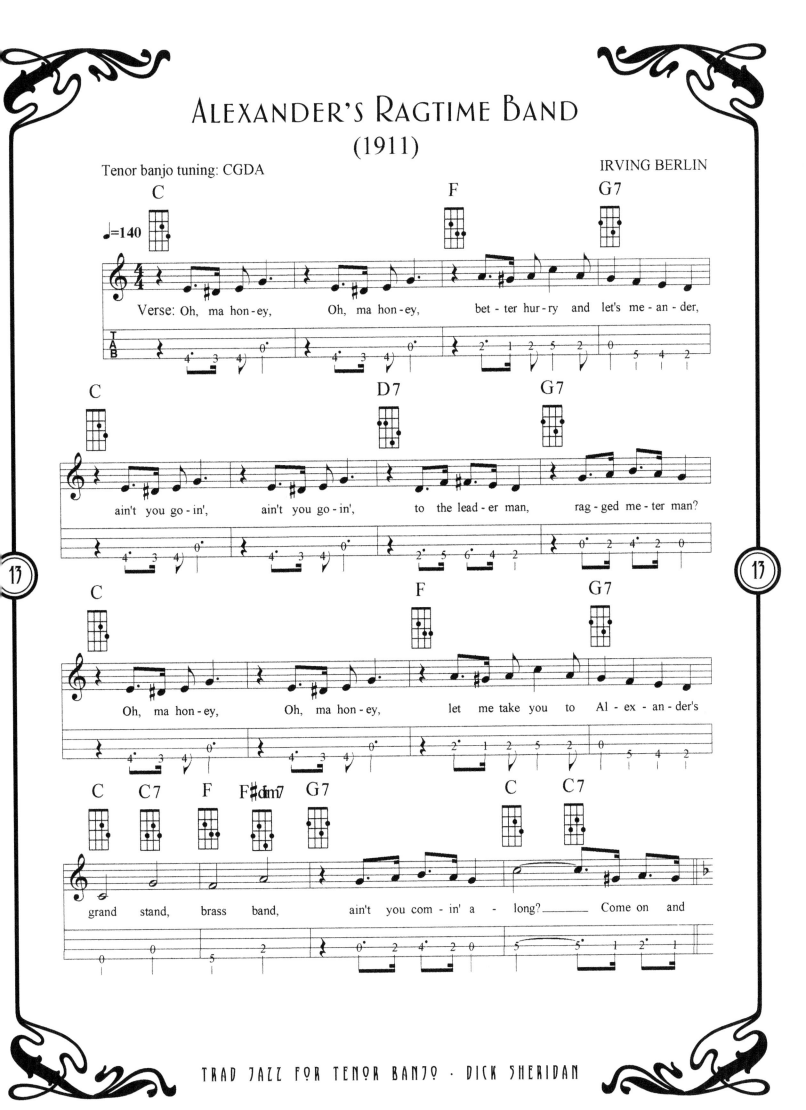

Alexander's Ragtime Band

A memory returns of playing with a group called Woody's Rubber Band. We held forth at a serviceman's club on a local military airbase, and "Alexander's Ragtime Band" was a regular song in our repertoire. I had never heard the verse before. Perhaps it was a few brews too many, but that night, sleep proved impossible. Musical demons were at work. I couldn't get that verse out of my head.

Alexander's Ragtime Band

Ragtime music was popular at the end of teh 19the century and continued on for another ten or twenty years. It certainly was in vogue when Berlin wrote this tune. But despite the song's syncopation - so characteristic of ragtime - and despite the song's title and lyrics - it's ironic that the song is not at all in the ragtime style. Note the key change from C to F when the verse goes to chorus.

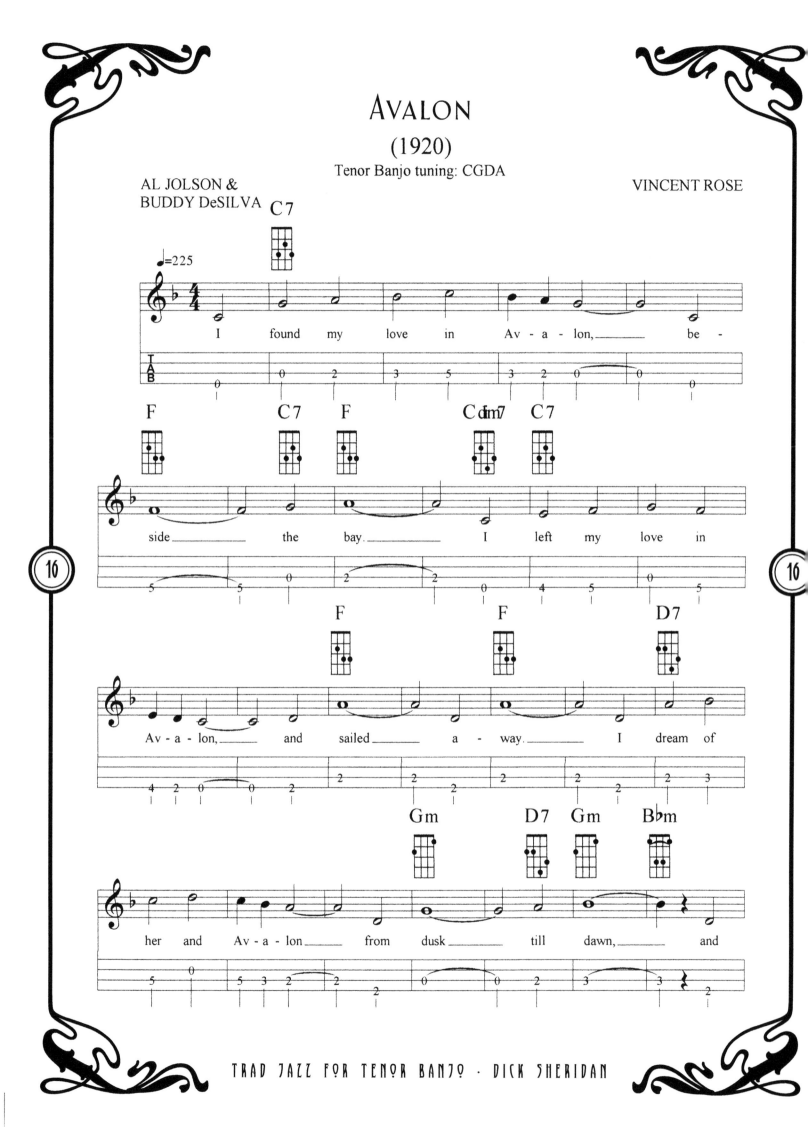

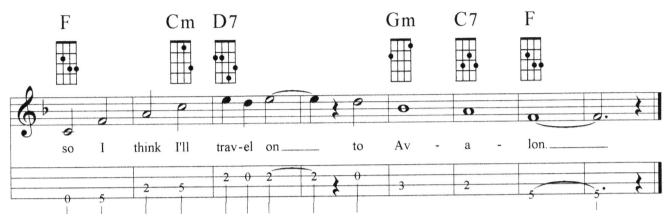

so I think I'll trav-el on_____ to Av - a - lon._____

Together with Vincent Rose and Buddy De Sylva, Al Jolson is listed as a co-composer, although his name might well have been added only to entice sales, a popular ploy of publishers at the time. Rose, a bandleader and prolific songwriter ("Whispering," "Linger Awhile," and "Blueberry Hill") in all probability wrote the music. De Sylva who was also one of Tin Pan Alley's top songwriters went on to co-found Capitol Records.

Baby, Won't You Please Come Home

(1919)

CHARLES WARFIELD

CLARENCE WILLIAMS

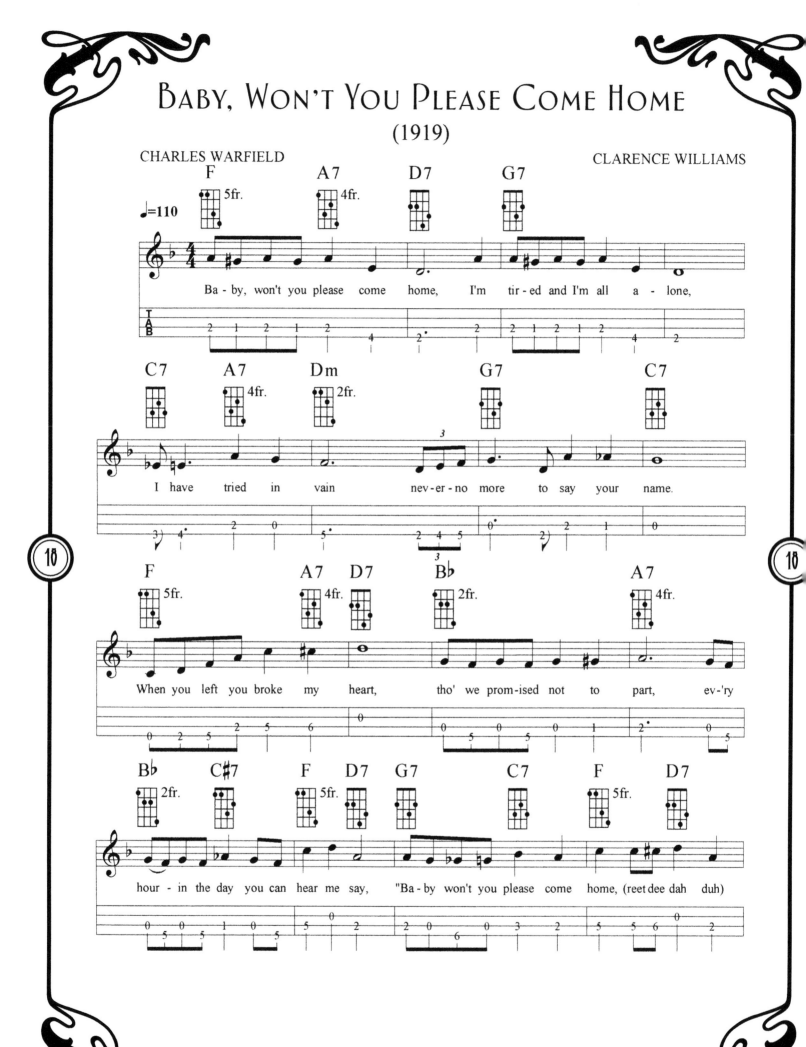

BABY, WON'T YOU PLEASE COME HOME

Charles Warfield claimed to be the sole author of this song. Clarence Williams published it and it was common practice for publishers at that time to put their names on the music as co-composers. Publishers felt that since they bore the expense of publication they should share in the royalties. As Williams put it, "If you couldn't get a piece of the copyright, it didn't pay to publish it."

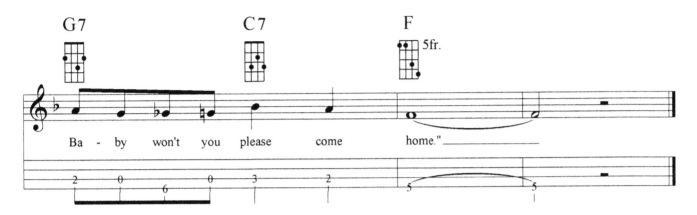

Ba - by won't you please come home." _____

My best friend from college days taught me this song, and this is the way he sang it, right or wrong. He had won a Kaiser car on a quiz show and in it we made the rounds of parties and goodtime events swapping songs and listening to the radio in search of new numbers to add to our collection.

It was this friend who introduced me to traditional jazz. I don't know how it came about, how he knew about this kind of music, but he did. He had accumulated a number of vintage recordings on tape of some of the best early New Orleans jazz bands and musicians; Bunk Johnson, Sidney Bechet, Kid Ory, King Oliver, Jelly Roll Morton, and the Original Dixieland Jazz Band.

Although I played ukulele and was just learning the tenor banjo, the only songs I knew were the pop tunes of the day and those from Tin Pan Alley that I heard my dad play on the piano. Hearing my friend's tapes opened the door to a new world of music that sparked an immediate fascination. It still continues - and has initiated a secondary career as an avocational professional musician.

There was a sound of the banjo on those tapes that is hard to duplicate or explain. I sometimes think it came from chords being played high on the fingerboard or perhaps it was just the style of those New Orleans players. Whatever, the sound is truly unique, a traditional voice that to my ear sounds "authentic."

While in college and much caught up in collegiate swagger, I happened to hear Wilbur de Paris and his New Orleans Jazz Band playing at Jimmy Ryan's jazz club in NYC on 52nd street. I was playing banjo by then with a campus group and took particular note of de Paris' banjo player, who was probably Eddie Gibbs, a versatile and highly accomplished musician. The club venue was long and narrow with the banjo player on the near end. I studied him intently and thought to myself what an easy life it must be to just sit and strum and not have a care in the world. How little did I know and how naive I was. Let me tell you, the good Lord has a sense of humor because there by the Grace of God that banjo player is now me.

BILL BAILEY
(1902)

Tenor Banjo tuning: CGDA

Hughie L. Cannon

Won't you come home, Bill Bail - ey, won't you come home?

She moans de whole day long,_____

I'll do de cook - ing, dar - ling, I'll pay de rent,

I know I'se done you wrong._____

TRAD JAZZ FOR TENOR BANJO · DICK SHERIDAN

BILL BAILEY

Here's an evergreen favorite that everyone seems to know, young and old. It's as popular on the bandstand as it is for house party sing-alongs and backyard barbeques. Hard to believe that the song is over 100 years old!

FAREWELL BLUES

(1922)

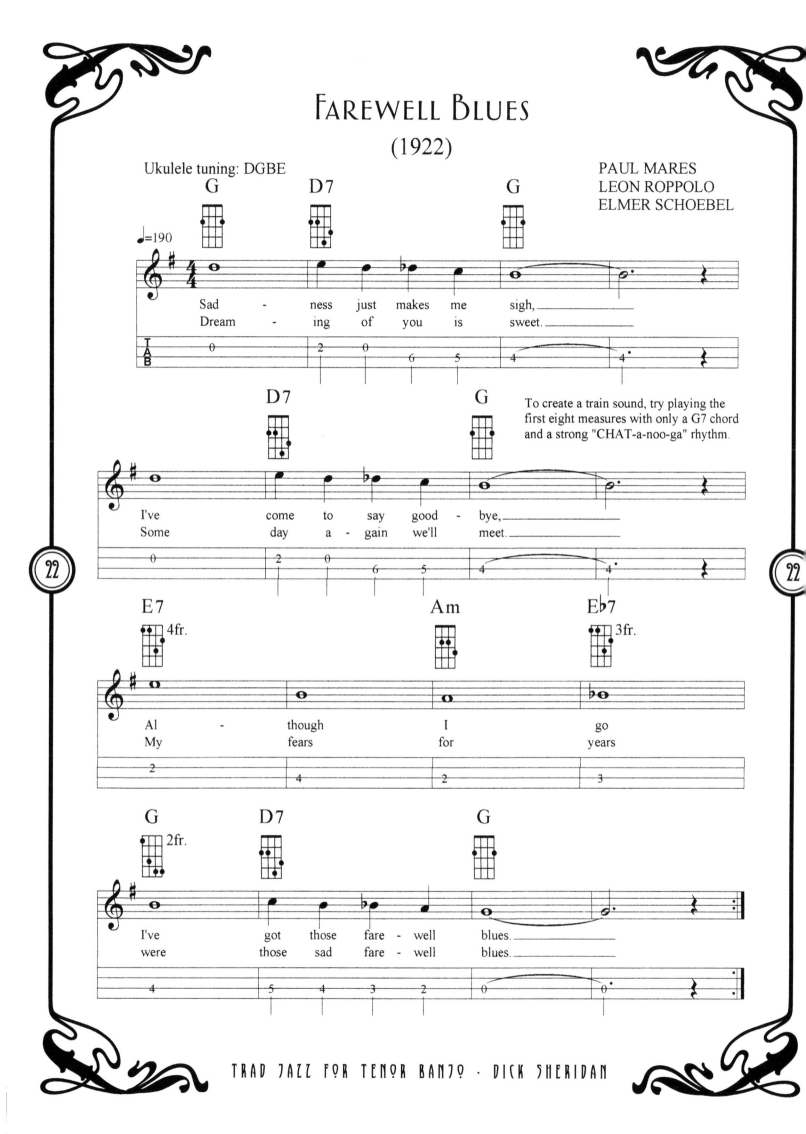

BLUEBELLS, GOODBYE
A march from the Spanish-American War

Tenor Banjo tuning: CGDA

Traditional

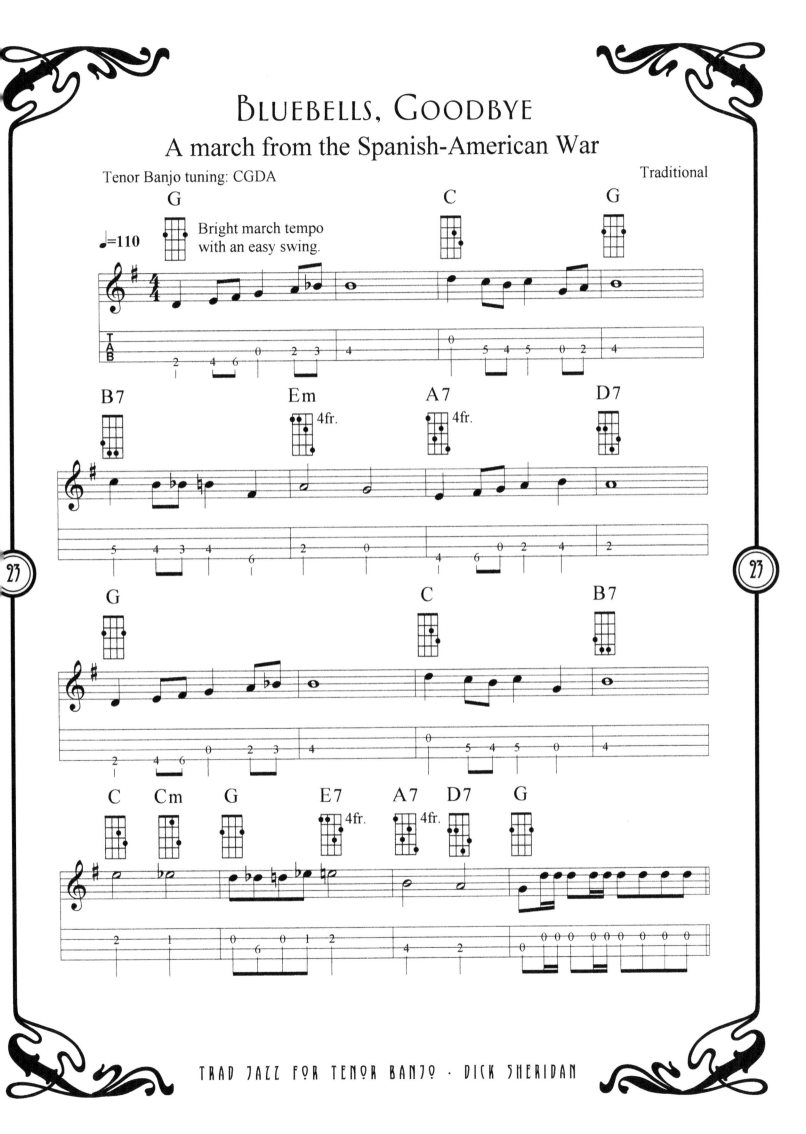

TRAD JAZZ FOR TENOR BANJO · DICK SHERIDAN

Bluebells, Goodbye

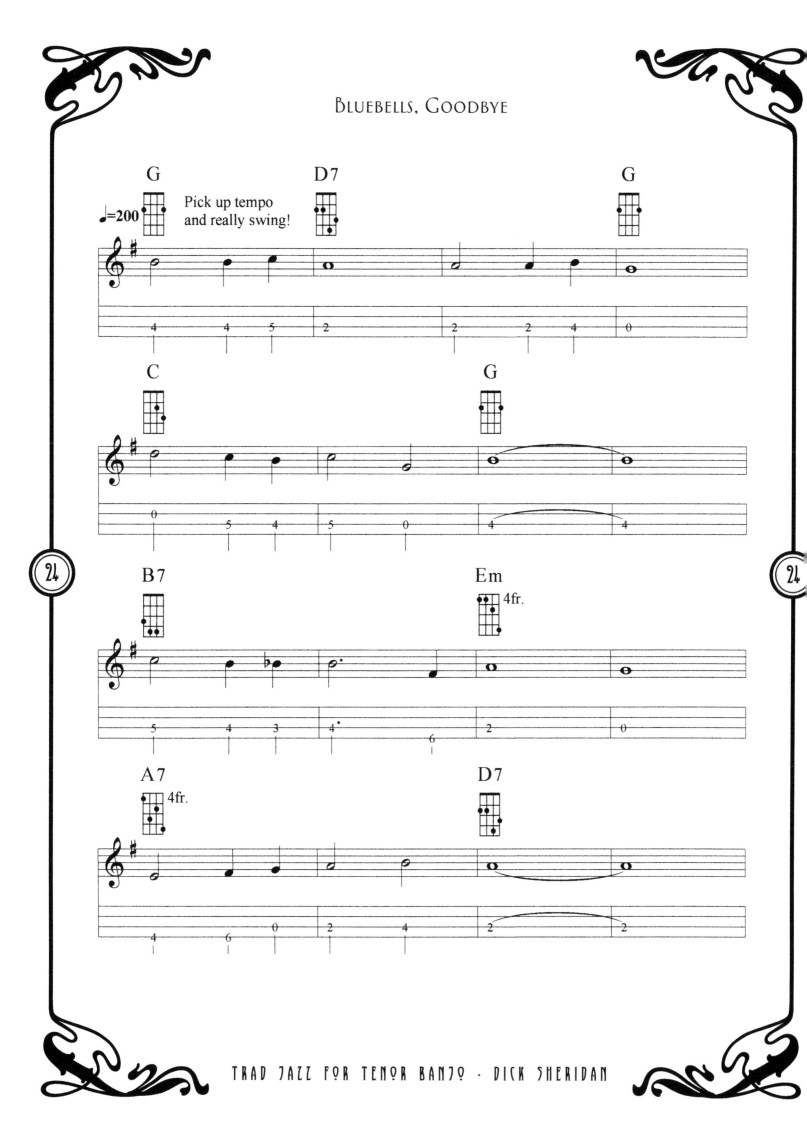

Bluebells, Goodbye

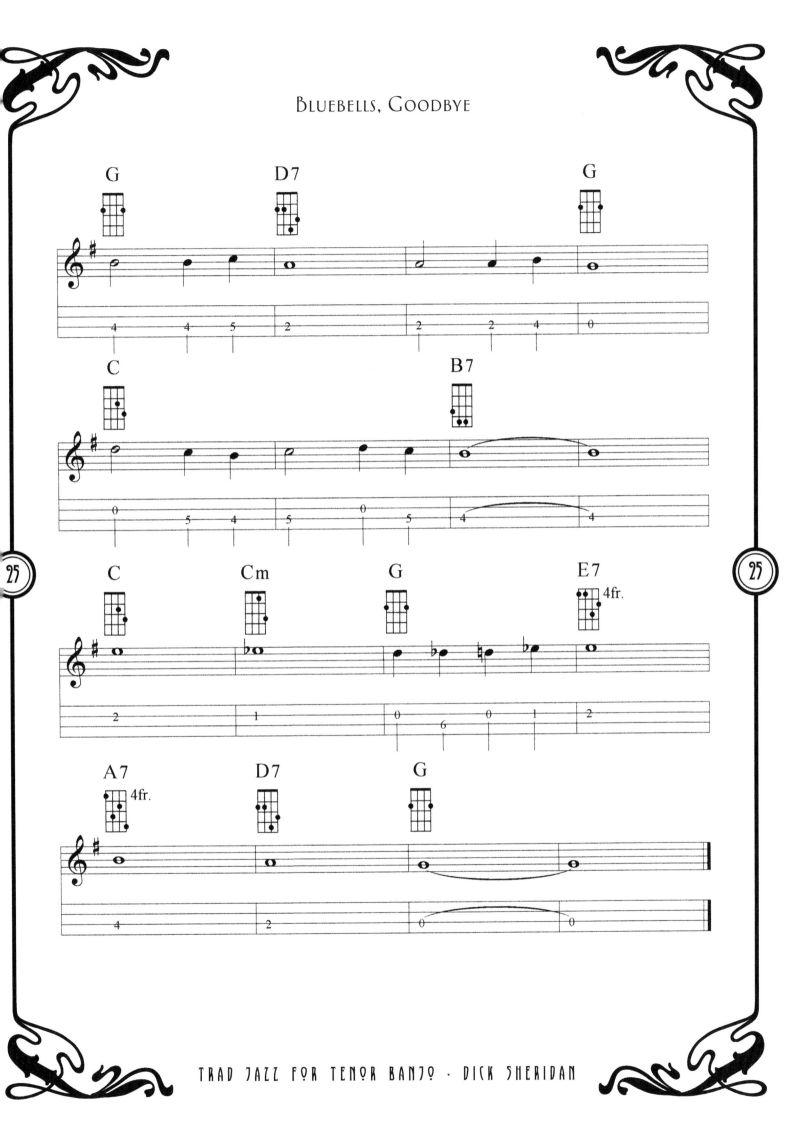

BY AND BY

Tenor Banjo tuning: CGDA

CHARLES A. TINDLEY

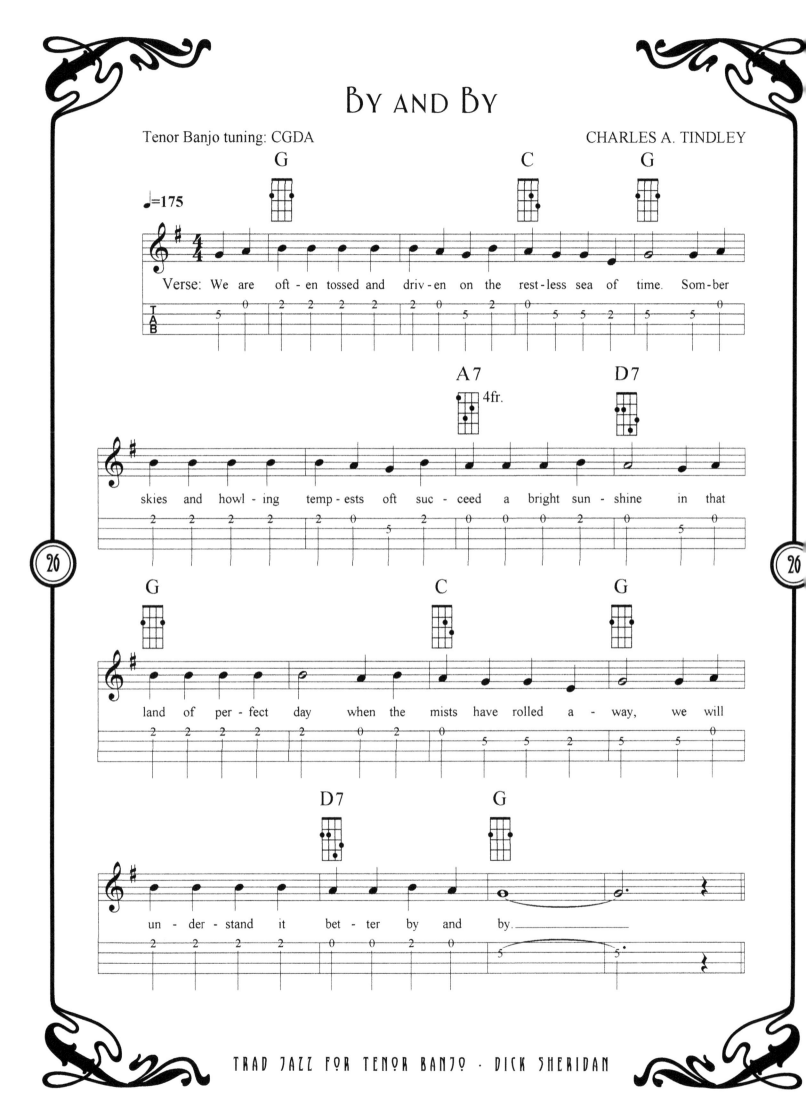

By and By

A popular spiritual played for both secular and religious occasions.

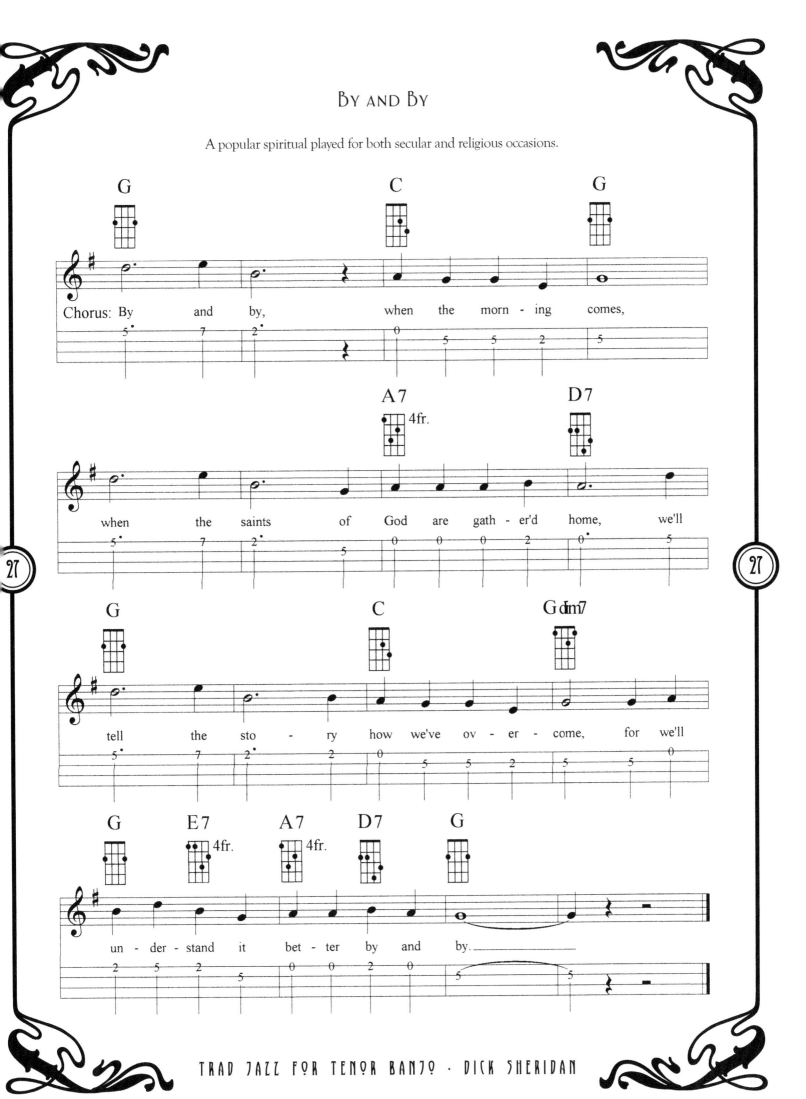

CHINA BOY
(1922)

Tenor Banjo tuning: CGDA

DICK WINFREE

PHIL BOUTELJE

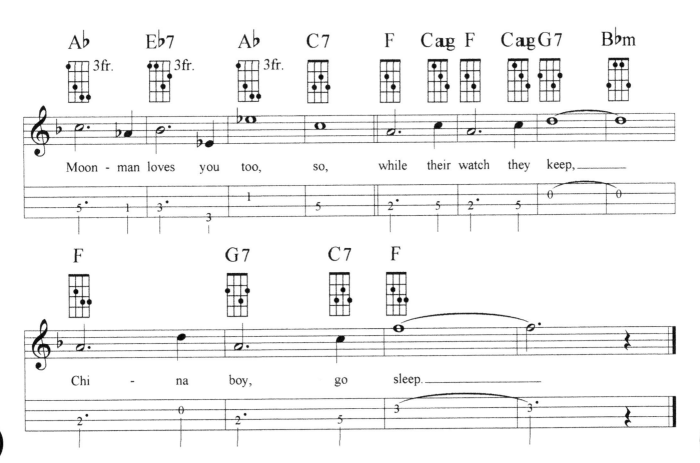

Moon - man loves you too, so, while their watch they keep,_____

Chi - na boy, go sleep._____

Because of the long holds on dotted half notes and tied whole notes, this song makes a great banjo chord solo. The key change to A-Flat adds interest and excitement. My band starts with the banjo and rhythm section playing a chorus, followed by an ensemble chorus and solos. The

banjo takes the last solo spot: two choruses, the first time ad lib and the second time straight chord melody. An ensemble chorus follows, then an 8-bar tag with the banjo playing a diminished chord run for the first 4 bars, the full band joining in for the last 4 measures.

HINDUSTAN
(1918)

HAROLD WEEKS   Tenor Banjo tuning: CGDA   OLIVER WALLACE

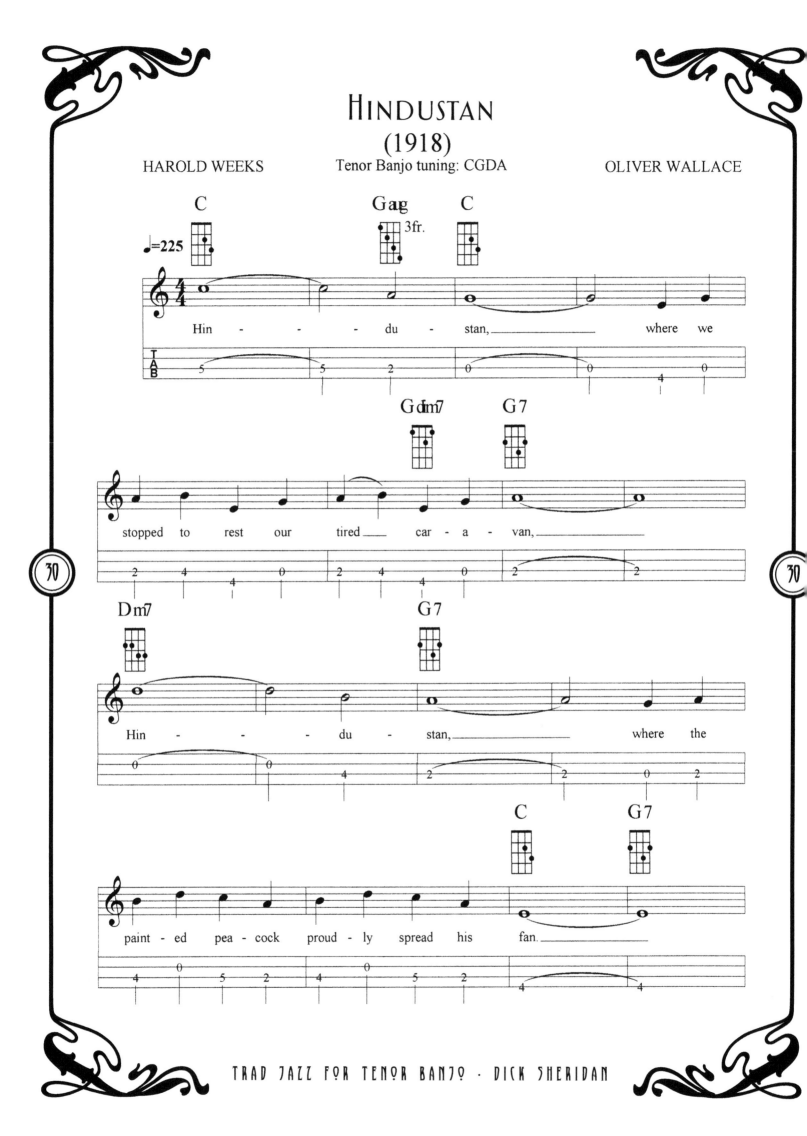

For many years there was a "Jazz at Noon" jam session at a local downtown hotel. Businessmen who were good amateur musicians would bring their instruments, take a break, and sit in. "Hindustan" was standard fare. I had trouble hearing the chord on the Ab note and asked our piano player what it was. "I don't know," he said, "I just play it." I positioned myself where I could watch his fingers (they were about the size of baby carrots) and eventually figured out that it was an Fm chord. Once learned, it has never been forgotten, but I must confess that I still have to think hard when that point in the song is reached.

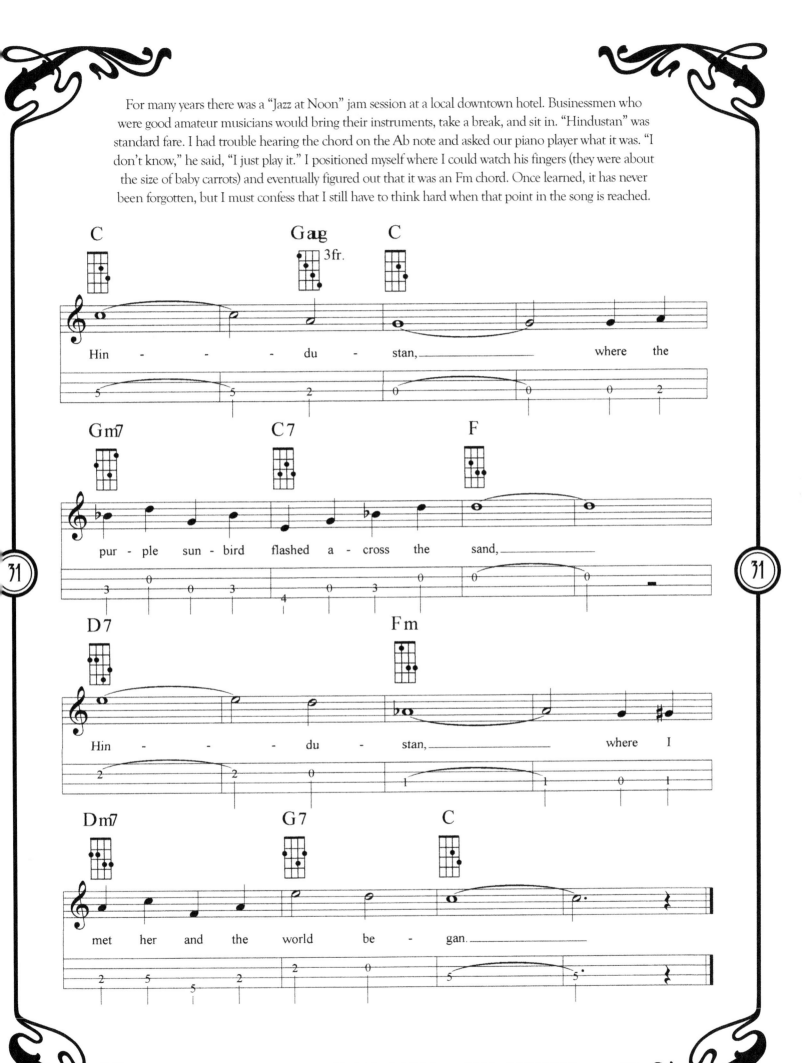

I Wish I Could Shimmy
Like My Sister Kate
(1919)

Tenor Banjo tuning: CGDA

A.J. PIRON

I wish I could shim-my like my sis-ter Kate, she shiv-ers like the jel-ly on a plate; my mam-my want-ed to know last night, why all the boys treat sis-ter Kate so nice. ___

E-Flat is the standard key for "Sister Kate." Although the chords are not a problem, the melody is a bit too demanding. To play in this key and use this arrangement, simply put a capo on the third fret.

I Wish I Could Shimmy Like My Sister Kate

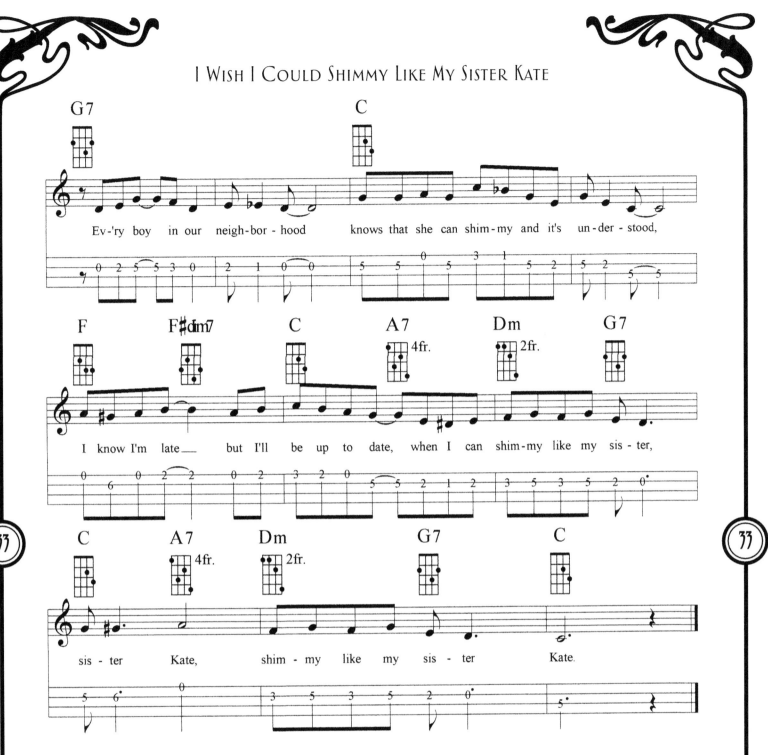

My college jazz band had been engaged to play for one of the Dartmouth fraternities in the mid-1950s. It was Winter Weekend and virtually all of the campus fraternities had a jazz band of their own. On Saturday morning there was a mini-concert featuring some of the bands. One group in particular sticks out in my mind, *The Very Seldom Jazz Band, Ltd.* from Brown University. Their banjo player was the personification of Joe College. His dark hair was close-cropped. He wore the classic uniform of those days - blue Oxford button-down shirt, narrow regimental rep tie, dark gray flannel trousers

with a buckle in the back, argyle socks, and white buck shoes. I remember he played a Bacon & Day "Silver Bell No. 1" tenor banjo. But what is more memorable is the song he sang, "I Wish I Could Shimmy Like My Sister Kate." It was the first time I had heard the song and I was mesmerized. Years later, I introduced the song to my own band and it became something of a signature song and vocal for me. It still is, although over the years the melody has been slightly modified and the words a little re-arranged. It's a great song, loaded with nostalgia, and a classic from the Roaring '20s.

I Was Floating Down
The Old Green River
(1915)
Tenor Banjo tuning: CGDA

BERT KALMER

JOE COOPER

I've been float - ing down the old green riv - er on the

good ship "Rock and Rye," _____ but I

float - ed too far, _____ I got stuck on a bar, _____ I was

out there a - lone _____ wish - ing that I was home. _____

The Old Green River

Husbands out on the town who come staggering home in the wee hours can certainly tell their wives some whoppers, but this one tops them all!

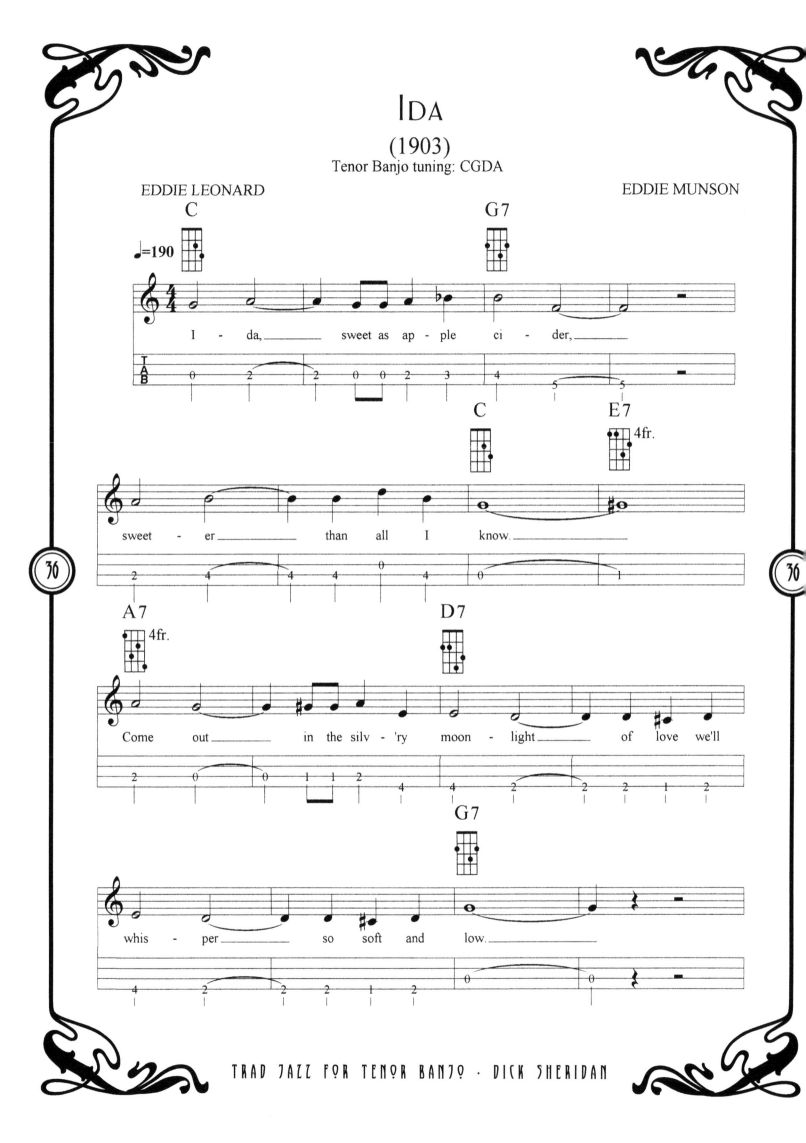

IDA

(1903)

Tenor Banjo tuning: CGDA

EDDIE LEONARD

EDDIE MUNSON

Ida

My band always gets confused between "Ida" and "Dinah." Just to set the record straight, this one is "Ida." The other one is not.

INDIANA

(1917)

Tenor Banjo tuning: CGDA

BALLARD MacDONALD

JAMES F. HANLEY

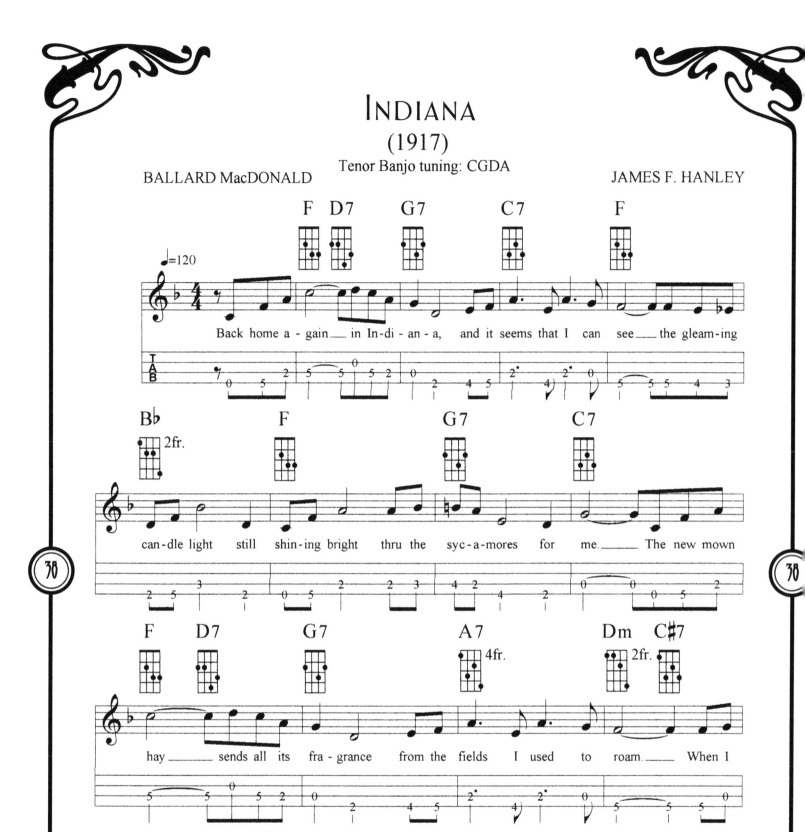

TRAD JAZZ FOR TENOR BANJO · DICK SHERIDAN

Indiana

Composer James Hanley, father of a childhood friend, passed away when his son and I were only in the 2nd grade. I recall seeing my friend's father just once, a stout man in a dark suit walking up from the Long Island Railroad station. He had a studio with a grand piano above the family's detached garage (which had a turntable to rotate the car), and as time went on, there my friend and I played, the studio musty and neglected, with music manuscript scattered about the floor. Other songs by James Hanley include, "Zing! Went the Strings of My Heart," "Rose of Washington Square," and "Second Hand Rose" with collaborator Ballard MacDonald providing the lyrics to several of his songs.

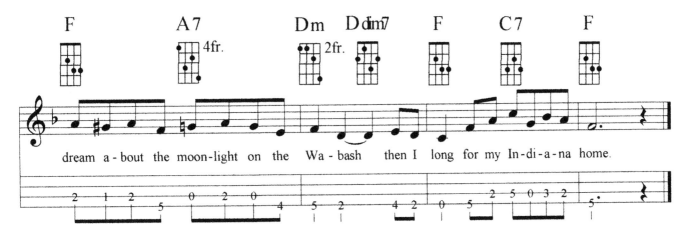

dream a-bout the moon-light on the Wa-bash then I long for my In-di-a-na home.

Although "On the Banks of the Wabash, Far Away" is the official state song of Indiana, the song "Indiana" has long been the unofficial favorite. Often identified by its opening words ("Back Home Again in Indiana") the song quotes at its conclusion several final bars of "Wabash." The Wabash River in Indiana was the inspiration for the state song written by Paul Dresser and first published in 1897. It was later adopted as the official state song in 1913. "Indiana" is traditionally played at the start of the annual Indianapolis 500 automobile race. Louis Armstrong liked the song so much that it was the concert opener for his All Star Band.

For the words and music of "On the Banks of the Wabash, Far Away," refer to Centerstream's NAUTICAL SONGS FOR UKULELE.

I think it fair to say that for traditional jazz bands, "Indiana" is probably the most popular standard of all time. The Original Dixieland Jazz Band recorded it on the Columbia label in 1917, the year of its publication. As such, it was one of the earliest jazz tunes to be recorded, and any band that has since made recordings will invariably have included the song in at least one of its issues.

Jazz Me Blues
(1921)

Tenor Banjo tuning: CGDA

TOM DELANEY

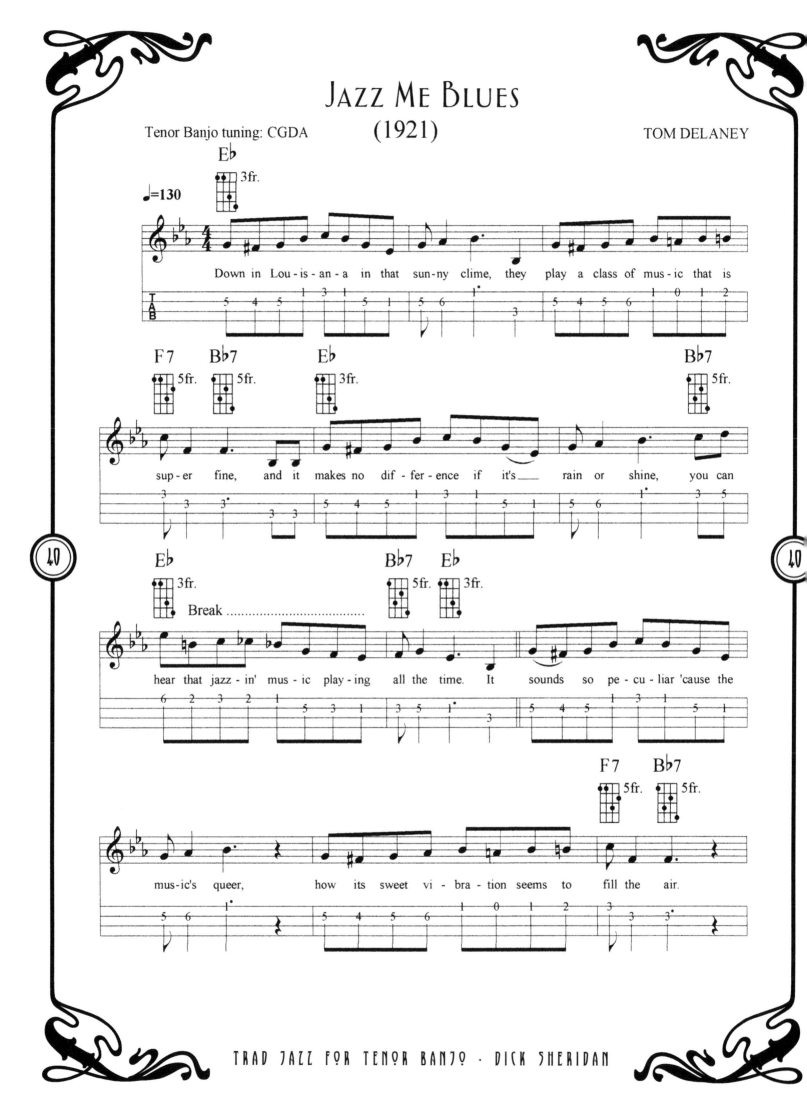

Jazz Me Blues

Jazz Me Blues

TRAD JAZZ FOR TENOR BANJO · DICK SHERIDAN

JAZZ. WHAT'S IN A NAME?

No word in the English language has a more obscure origin than the word, "Jazz." Some word detectives claim its history goes back to before the Civil War. The initial root they say is "jism" whose meaning appears to be peppy, spirited, energetic. Along came the derivitive "jasm" and from there, it was a hop, skip and jump to "jazz" and its alternate form, "jass."

The word seems to have been popular as slang on the West Coast as early as 1912. But it was banjoist Bert Kelly who may have been one of the first to use it in a musical context when he applied the term to his Chicago-based group in 1915 known as *Bert Kelly's Jazz Band.*

Two years later an article in the New Orleans Times-Picayune made reference to "jas bands," and it was about this time when the name started to circulate, witness the appearance of the celebrated Original Dixieland Jazz Band.

There are those who maintain that the word "jazz" has unsavory connotations and initially was unfit for polite society. True or not, the word is unblemished today. It's here to stay and it pops up everywhere - jazz bands, jazz clubs, jazz festivals, jazz dancing, jazzy fashions, Dixieland Jazz, modern jazz, progressive jazz, and an infinite number of items jazzed up.

But as for the evolution of the word - when all is said and done and the etymologists, academics and lexiconographers all have had their fun - the mystery continues and the word's original meaning still remains unclear, elusive and ever-more shall be so.

Make Me a Pallet on Your Floor

Tenor Banjo tuning: CGDA

TRADITIONAL

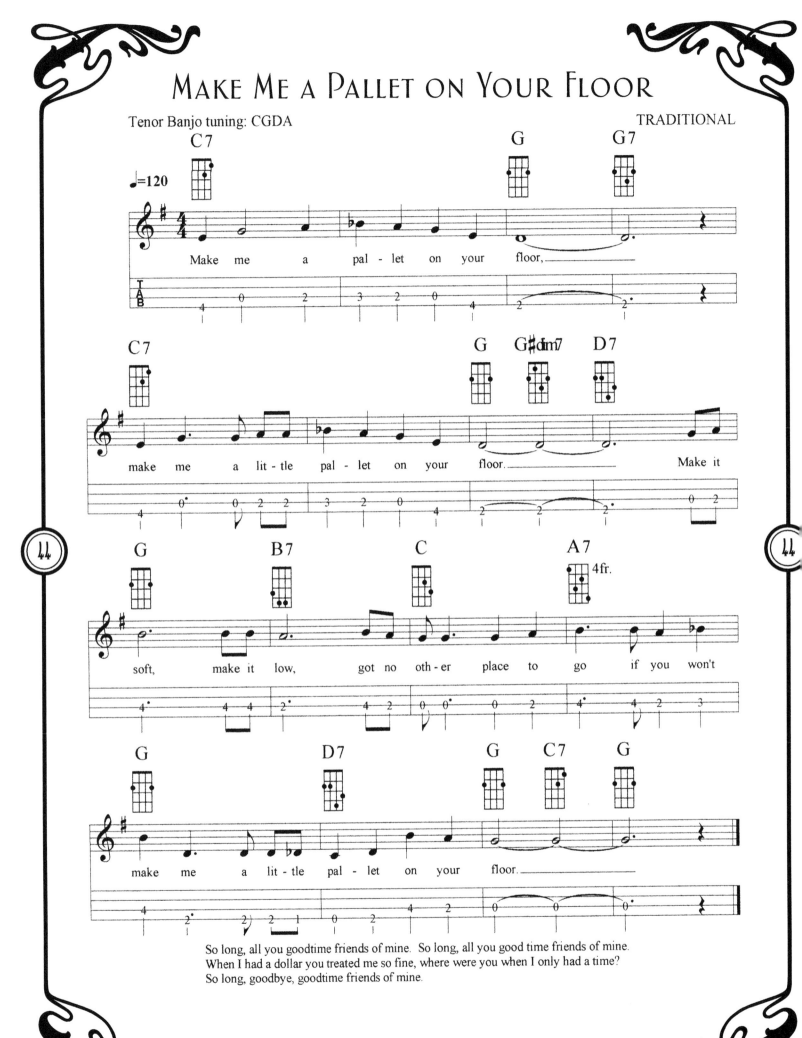

So long, all you goodtime friends of mine. So long, all you good time friends of mine.
When I had a dollar you treated me so fine, where were you when I only had a time?
So long, goodbye, goodtime friends of mine.

TRAD JAZZ FOR TENOR BANJO · DICK SHERIDAN

Just a Little While To Stay Here
(1921)

Tenor Banjo tuning: CGDA

E.M. BARTLETT

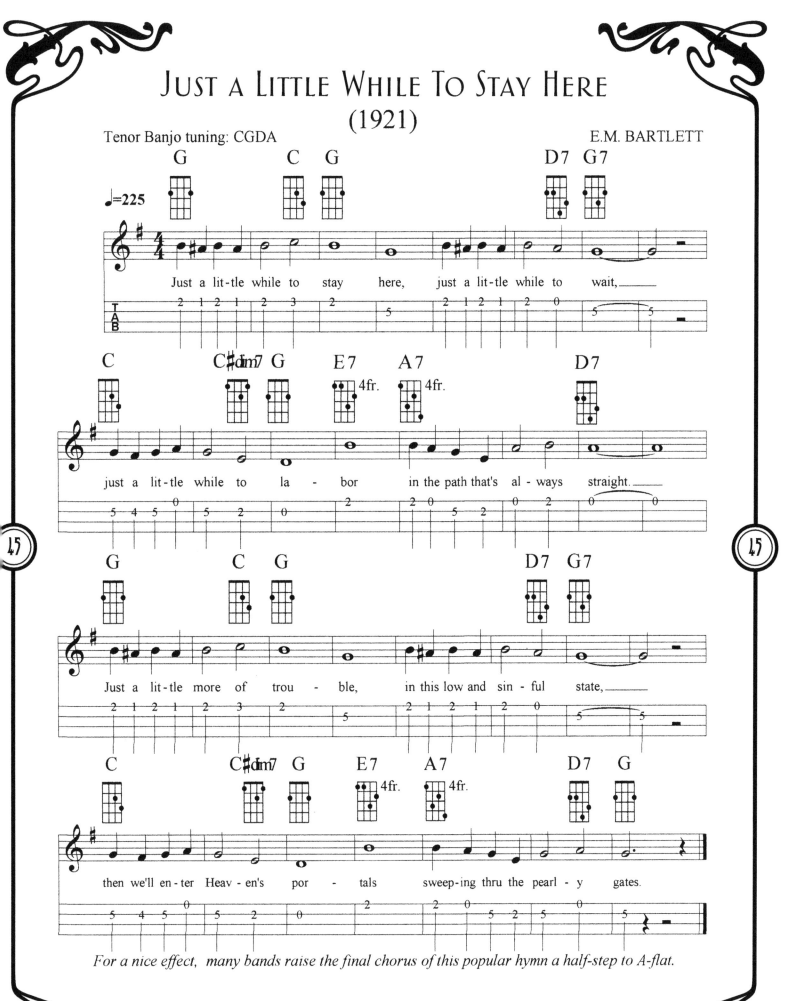

For a nice effect, many bands raise the final chorus of this popular hymn a half-step to A-flat.

45

MARGIE
(1920)

Tenor Banjo tuning: CGDA

BENNY DAVIS

CON CONRAD &
J. RUSSEL ROBINSON

My lit - tle Mar - gie, I'm al - ways think-ing of you,

Mar - gie, I'll tell the world I love you, don't for - get your

prom-ise to me,_____ I have bought a house and ring and ev - 'ry thing for

Margie

"Margie" was introduced in December of 1920 on a Victor label record by The Original Dixieland Jazz Band. The band's pianist J. Russell Robinson is listed as co-composer. Eddie Cantor's young daughter was the inspiration for the song's title.

The cyclic sequence of chords in measures 24 and 25 (A7-D7-G7-C7) is heard on the ODJB recording and is especially worthwhile to add to your playing with whatever chord inversions you choose.

MIDNIGHT IN MOSCOW

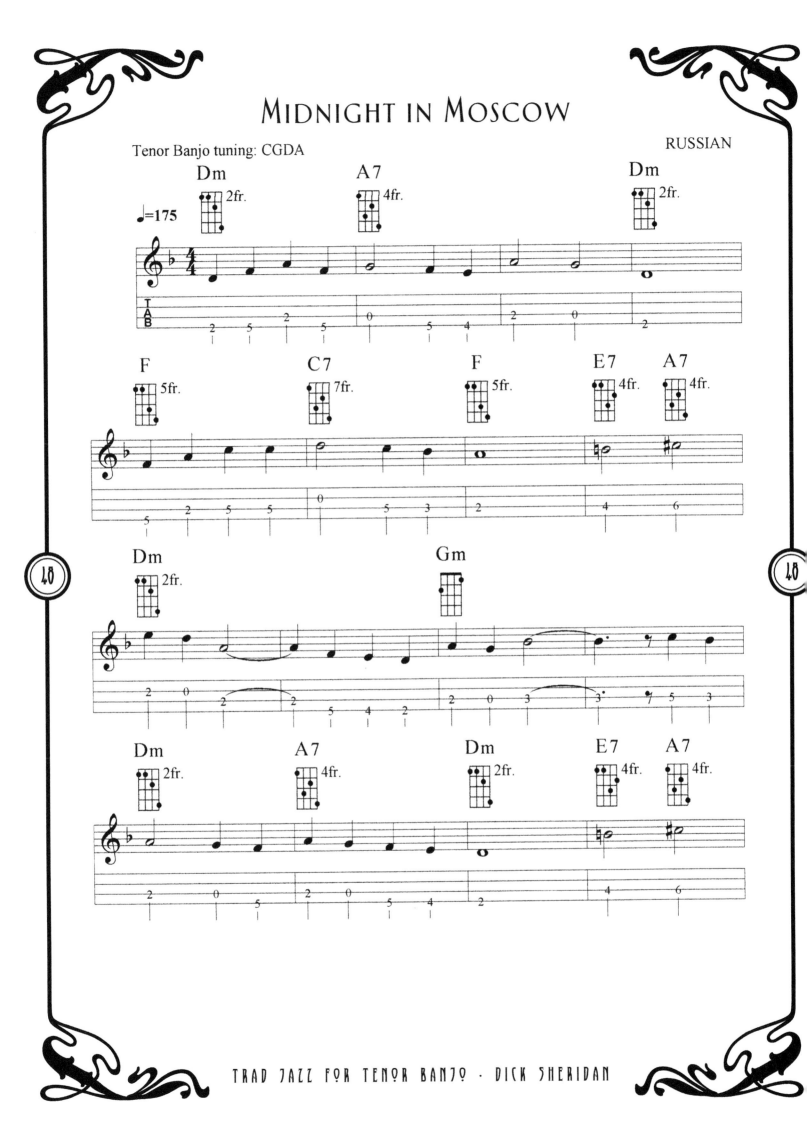

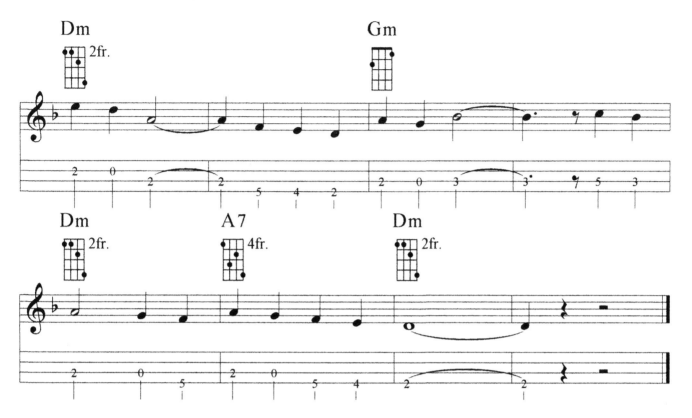

Originally known as "Moscow Nights," the song was recorded by Kenny Ball & His Jazzmen, a British jazz group, under the title of "Midnight in Moscow." It was on top of the charts for eleven weeks, hitting the number 2 spot in March of 1962. The Kenny Ball arrangement started in Cm then climbed up to Dm and Fm. Unlike most of the early banjoists who played sitting down, Ball's banjo player stood, as did many during the folk boom of the '60s and '70s, as some do today.

Oh, Didn't He Ramble

(1906)

Tenor Banjo tuning: CGDA

WILL HANDY

♩=110 Slow march tempo en route to the cemetery.

Oh, Didn't He Ramble

Returning from the cemetery.
Upbeat with an easy swing.

♩=200

ram - ble, ram - ble, he ram-bled all a - round, up and down the town, oh, did-n't he ram - ble, ram - ble, he ram-bled till the butch-er cut him down,

One of the unique traditions of New Orleans is the so-called jazz funeral, although many from that city would rather refer to it as simply a funeral procession "with music." On the way to the cemetery, the hearse is followed by walking mourners and a jazz band playing doleful hyms and dirges. After the deceased has been committed to a final resting place and the preacher concludes with "ashes to ashes and dust to dust," the brethren leave the cemetery and a hymn like "Saints" or "Closer Walk" is played. But then the mood changes. The somber pall is lifted and there's a spirit of rejoicing. The deceased has moved on to a better place, we trust, and it's time to celebrate life. The band starts to swing and shift to upbeat spirituals and tunes. Those following the band - the mourners and bystanders called the "second line" - dance and gyrate, parasols are twirled, handkerchiefs waved. The deceased is fondly remembered: "Oh! Didn't He Ramble!" ... and life goes on.

TRAD JAZZ FOR TENOR BANJO · DICK SHERIDAN

Runnin' Wild

(1922)

Tenor Banjo tuning: CGDA

JOE GREY & LEO WOOD

A. H. GIBBS

Runnin' Wild

You may recall the train scene from the movie *Some Like It Hot*, where Marilyn Monroe dressed in slinky black is strumming a ukulele and singing "Runnin' Wild." She was part of an all-girl orchestra en route to a gig in California at the Hotel Del Coronado. The band was playing in the key of F, Marilyn changed keys to Eb, the original sheet music was in Bb, and my band plays it in the key of C.

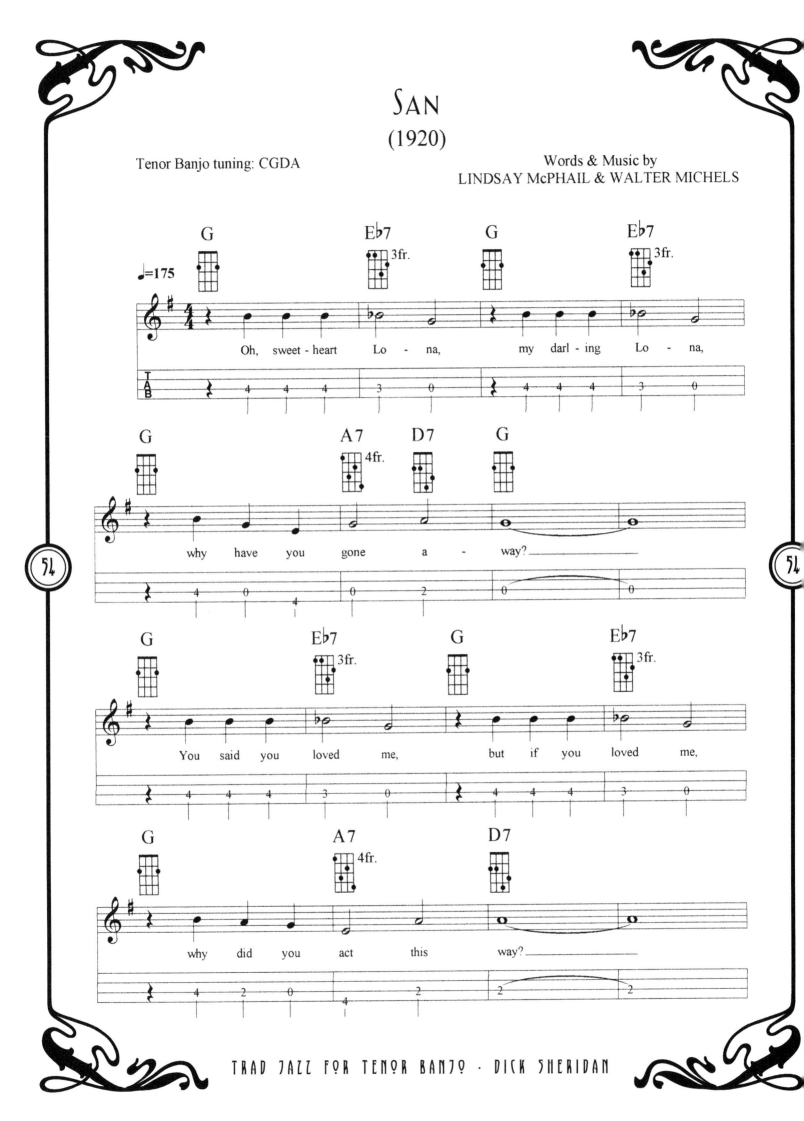

TRAD JAZZ FOR TENOR BANJO · DICK SHERIDAN

San

Verse: "King San of Senegal sat on the shore at Bulamay singing a sad refrain to his dear Queen (Lona) who'd gone away..." For a full band recording, check out www.HalcyonDaysMusic.com. The site is dedicated to the webmaster's Scottish grandfather "who played tenor banjo in a dance band for social events on a rubber plantation estate in Malaya during the 1920s."

THE SHEIK OF ARABY

(1921)

Tenor Banjo tuning: CGDA

TED SNYDER

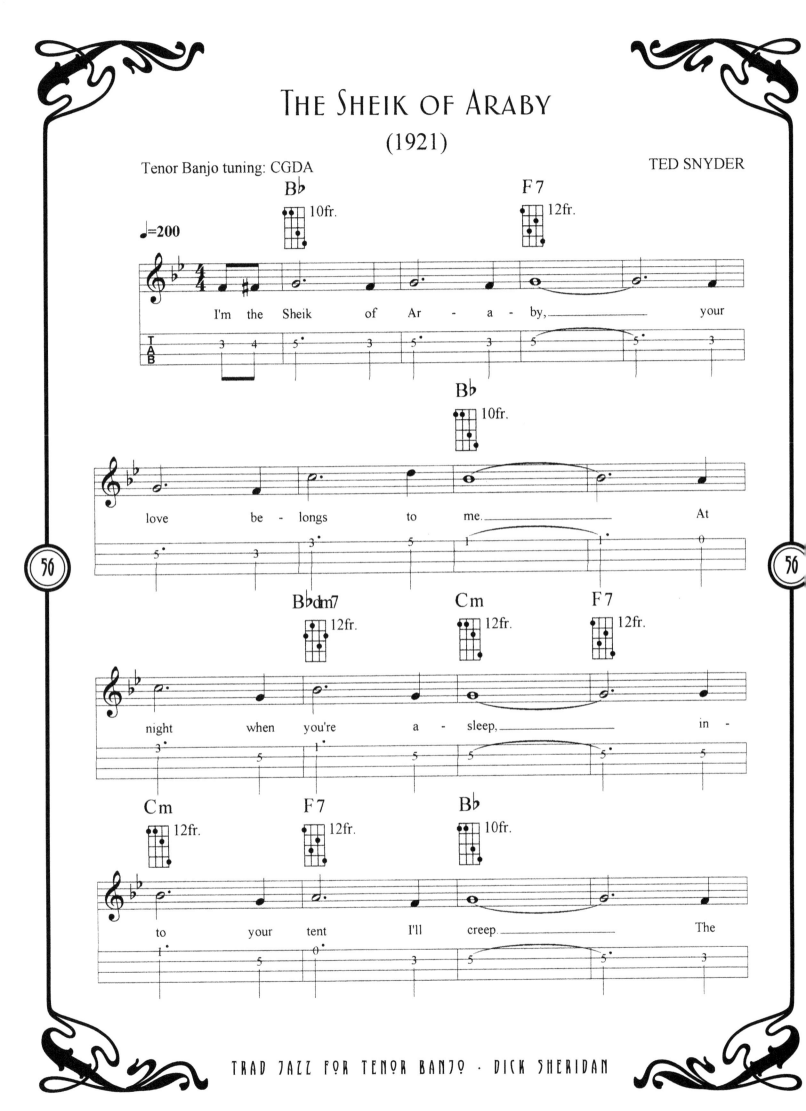

THE SHEIK OF ARABY

The 1921 movie "The Sheik" starring Rudolph Valentino was the inspiration for this song. Jazz bands, especially in New Orleans, picked up on the film's popularity, and the song has remained a classic in the trad jazz repetoire. Woody Allen's band was playing the song at Michael's Pub in NYC the night it was announced that he had won the Best Picture Oscar in 1977 for "Annie Hall." I've been told that Woody just kept playing and never missed a beat.

YELLOW DOG BLUES
(1912)

Tenor Banjo tuning: CGDA

W.C. HANDY

TRAD JAZZ FOR TENOR BANJO · DICK SHERIDAN

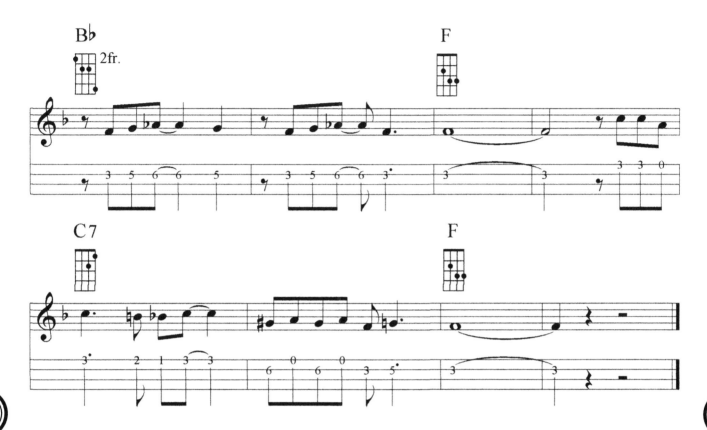

59

Originally titled "The Yellow Dog Rag," and subtitled "Where the Southern Crosses the Yellow Dog," a reference to the intersection of the Southern Railroad intersecting with the Yazoo & Mississippi Valley Railroad, the latter known locally as the "Yellow Dog." Despite the song having no reference to actual canines, when the break comes in the second part, the audience loves to imitate all forms of dog sounds — howls & growls, barks & woofs, and any other dog yelps that come to mind. Pandemonium, for sure, but lots of fun in the process.

Note: Each section of the song is usually repeated. Play A twice and B twice. The key change in the B part has been added somewhere along the line. It was not in Handy's original score.

Historic site "Where the Southern Crosses the Yellow Dog" in Moorhead, Mississippi.

SMILES

(1917)

Tenor Banjo tuning: CGDA

J. WILL CALLAHAN

LEE S. ROBERTS

Smiles

"Smiles" is a great favorite from the days of World War I, having been written just as the United States entered the war. Its popularity continued with the early jazz players, and it remains a standard to this day.

With a simple, straightforward chord progression, it's a relaxing song to play, arranged here with mostly lower-fret open-string chords. Lee Roberts supposedly wrote the tune on the back of a cigarette package

Some of These Days

(1910)

Tenor Banjo tuning: CGDA

SHELTON BROOKS

SOME OF THESE DAYS

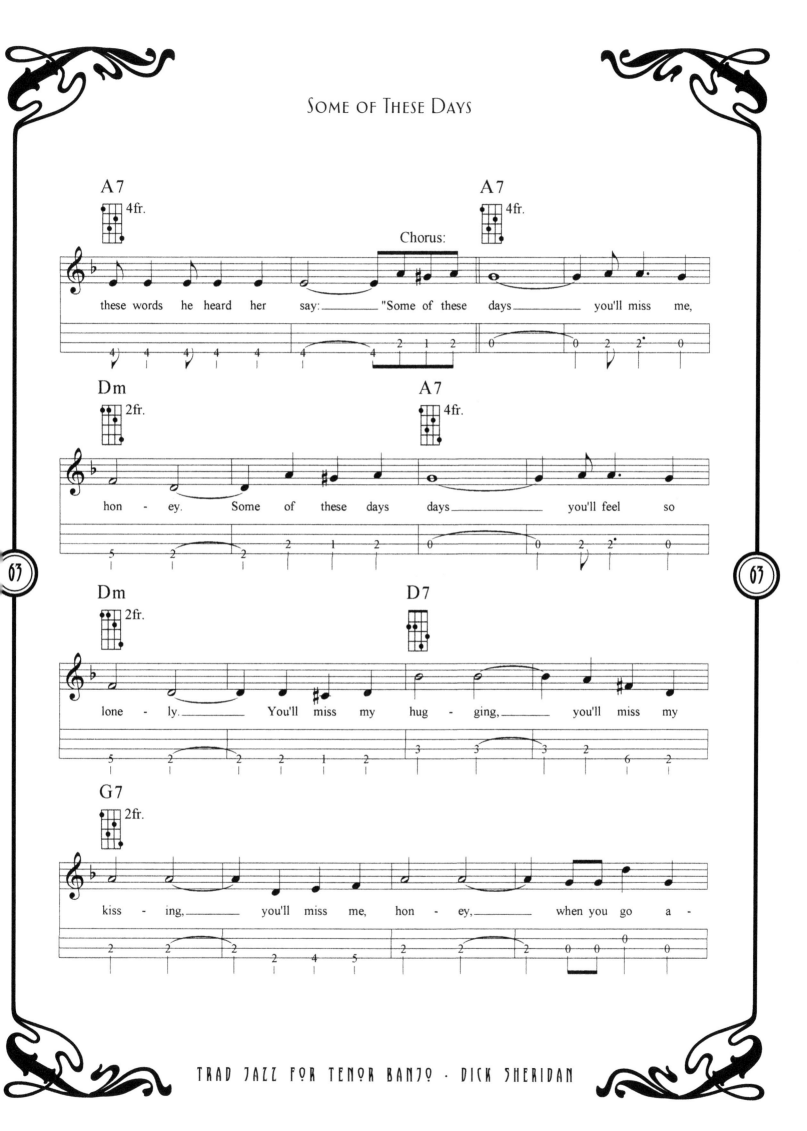

Some of These Days

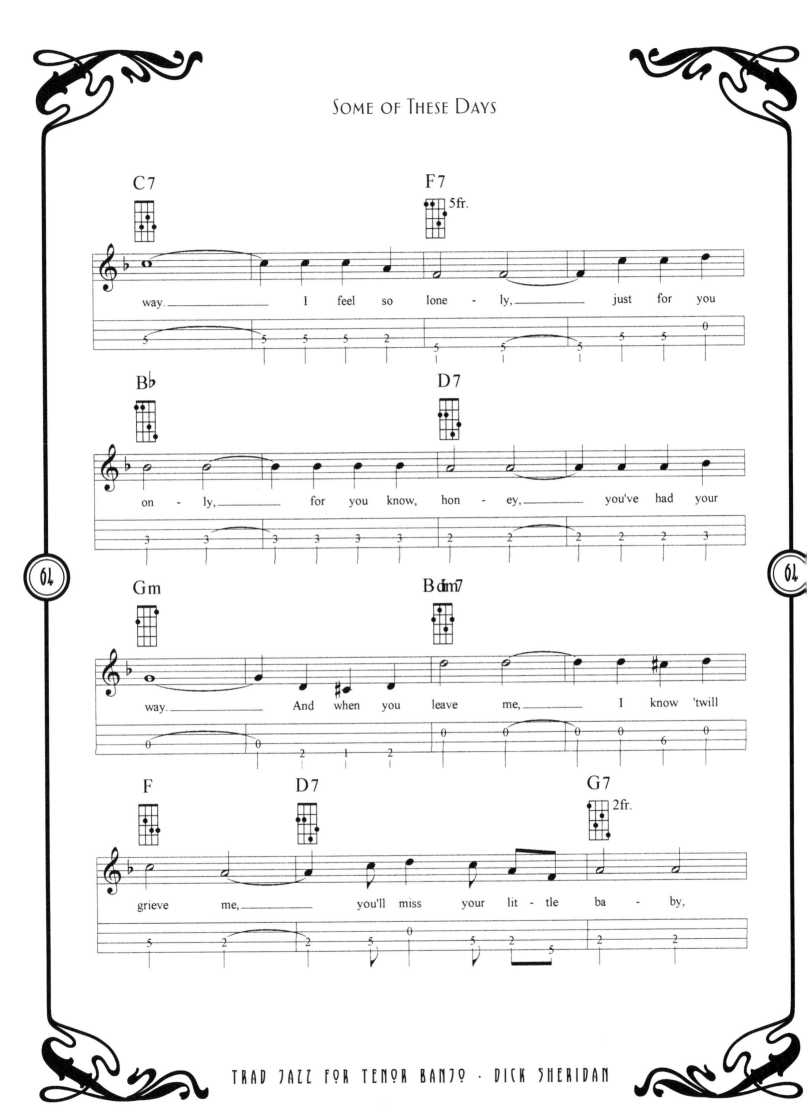

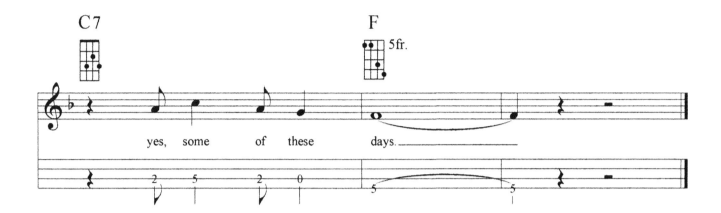

yes, some of these days.

Sophie Tucker, a prominent vaudeville and stage star - actress, singer and comedian - first recorded this song shortly after it was published in 1910 and then again in 1927 when it proved a huge hit and became her signature number. Born in Russia, she was the daughter of a Jewish family that emigrated to America, settled in Connecticut, and opened a restaurant where Sophie began her singing career by serenading the customers. Sophie was a large woman who wore gigantic hats and draped herself in floor-length, loose-fitting gowns to conceal her ample girth. Her voice was powerful and brash. With a repetoire that included both comical and suggestive songs, she was known as "The Last of the Red Hot Mamas." In deference to Sophie, the lyrics in the final few measures are often changed to "You'll miss your Red Hot Mama some one of these days," although Sophie herself often substituted the words "big fat mama."

When I was a young teenager, my father who was a native New Yorker and knew the City well took me one afternoon to the Metropole Cafe on 7th Ave. and 48th Street. Back of the bar there was a long runway where bands performed. That afternoon, a stout woman dressed like Sophie Tucker and accompanied only by a piano was belting out some of Sophie's well-known songs. My dad ordered a beer, and I was given one too - in a shot glass. The music and saloon ambience were exciting to me, and I'm sure that was the first time I had ever been in a pub or heard "Some of These Days."

The Metropole Cafe for many years was the scene for both traditional and modern jazz. It featured both afternoon and evening performances. The brief one I experienced standing at the bar with my father was unforgettable, and that memory stays with me vividly to this day.

Cynthia Sayer -
Jazz Banjoist, Vocalist,
Recording Artist,
Entertainer, and
2006 Inductee into the
National Four-String
Banjo Hall of Fame.

St. James Infirmary

Tenor Banjo tuning: CGDA

Traditional

TRAD JAZZ FOR TENOR BANJO · DICK SHERIDAN

St. Louis Blues
(1914)

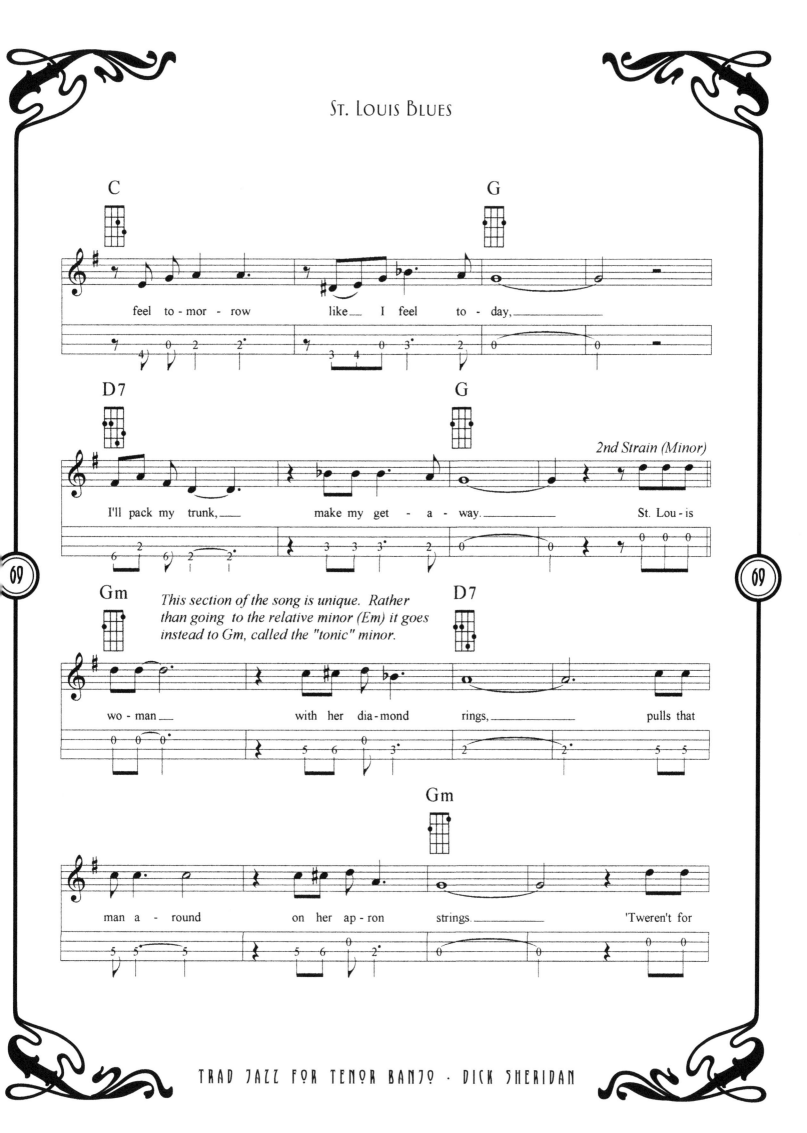

This section of the song is unique. Rather than going to the relative minor (Em) it goes instead to Gm, called the "tonic" minor.

St. Louis Blues

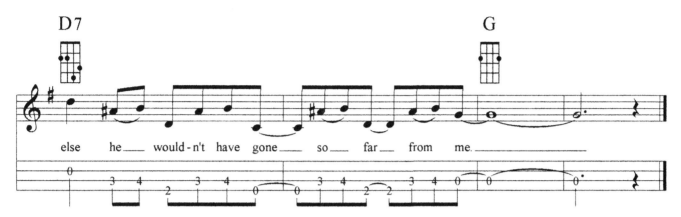

else he would-n't have gone so far from me.

1st Strain: Been to the Gypsy to get my fortune told,
To the Gypsy, done got my fortune told.
'Cause I'm most wild 'bout my Jelly Roll.
Gypsy done told me, "Don't you wear no black."
Yes, she done told me "Don't you wear no black."
"Go to St. Louis, you can win him back."

2nd Strain (Minor): Help me to Cairo, make St. Louis myself,
Git to Cairo, find my old friend Jeff.
Gwine to pin myself close to his side,
If I flag his train, I sure can ride.

3rd Strain: I loves that man like a school boy loves his pie,
Like a Kentucky Col'nel loves his mint and rye.
I'll love my baby till the day I die.

Alternate 3rd Strain: A black headed gal make a freight train jump the track,
Said a black headed gal make a freight train jump the track.
But a red headed woman makes a preacher Ball the Jack.

Alternate 3rd Strain: Lawd, a blonde headed woman makes a good man leave the town.
I said blonde headed woman makes a good man leave the town.
But a red headed woman makes a boy slap his papa down.

Alternate 3rd Strain: Oh, ashes to ashes and dust to dust,
I said ashes to ashes and dust to dust,
If my blues don't get you my jazzing must.

71

Tishomingo Blues
(1917)

Tenor Banjo tuning: CGDA

SPENCER WILLIAMS

I'm goin' to Tish-o-min-go be-cause I'm sad to day,____

I wish to lin-ger way down old Dix-ie way. ____

Oh! my wear-y heart cries out in pain, Oh! how I wish that I was back a-gain,

with a race____ in a place____ where they make you wel-come all the time. Way

TRAD JAZZ FOR TENOR BANJO · DICK SHERIDAN

Tishomingo Blues

For those like me who are geographically challenged, were it not for the lyrics I would never have known that Tishomingo is located in the state of Mississippi. Garrison Keillor has adopted the tune (key of D) with a change in lyrics for his radio broadcast, *A Prairie*

Home Companion: "I hear that old piano from down the avenue..." Both composer Spencer Williams and his brother Clarence Williams have contributed a significant number of standards to the trad jazz repertoire.

TRAD JAZZ FOR TENOR BANJO · DICK SHERIDAN

WABASH BLUES
(1921)

Tenor Banjo tuning: CGDA

DAVE RINGLE

FRED MEINKEN

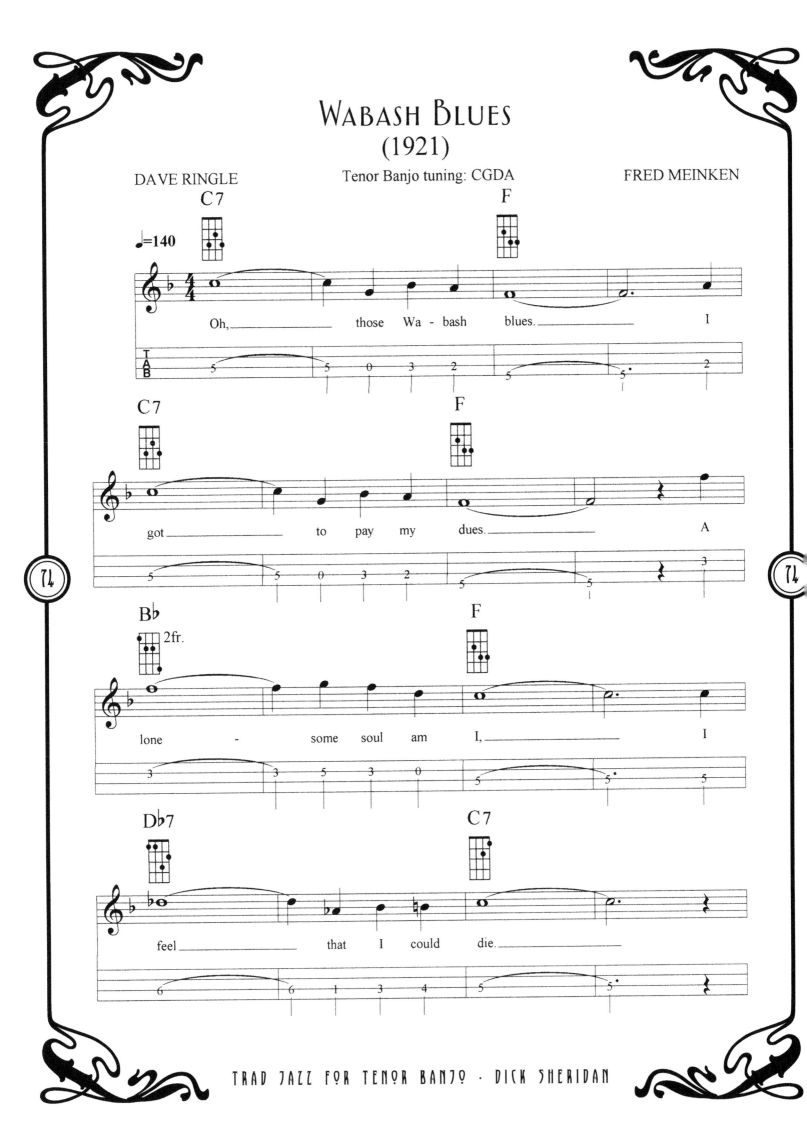

WABASH BLUES

Isham Jones and his Orchestra topped the charts with this popular jazz standard in 1921. It remained on the charts for 12 weeks, held the #1 spot for six of them, and sold over two million copies. Jones also wrote the music for "I'll See You in My Dreams" and "It Had to Be You."

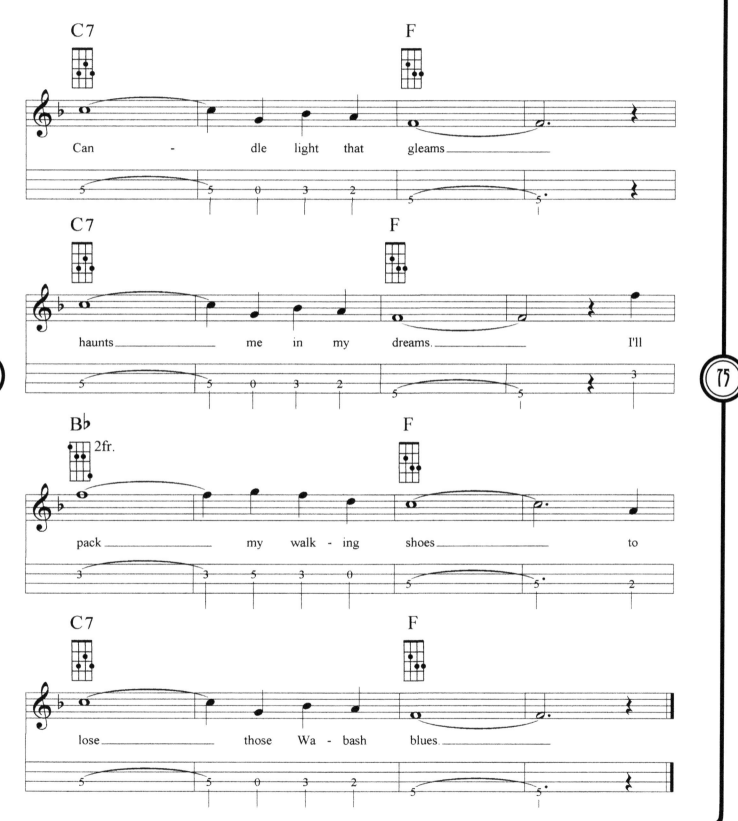

Way Down Yonder in New Orleans

(1922)

Tenor Banjo tuning: CGDA

HENRY CREAMER

JOHN T. LAYTON

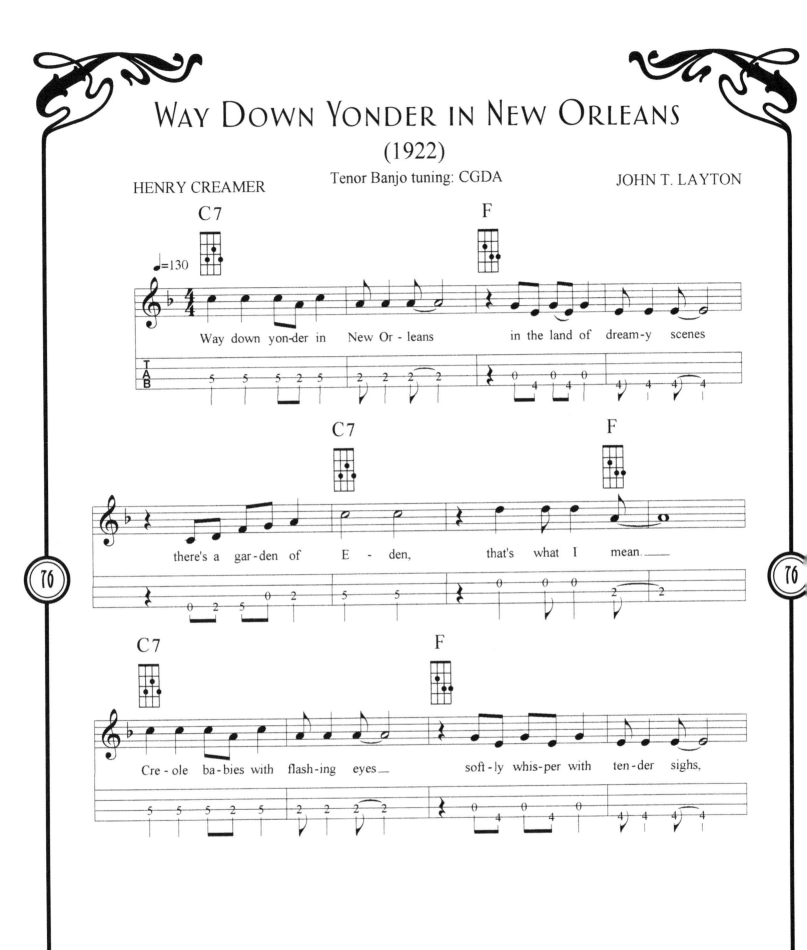

Way Down Yonder in New Orleans

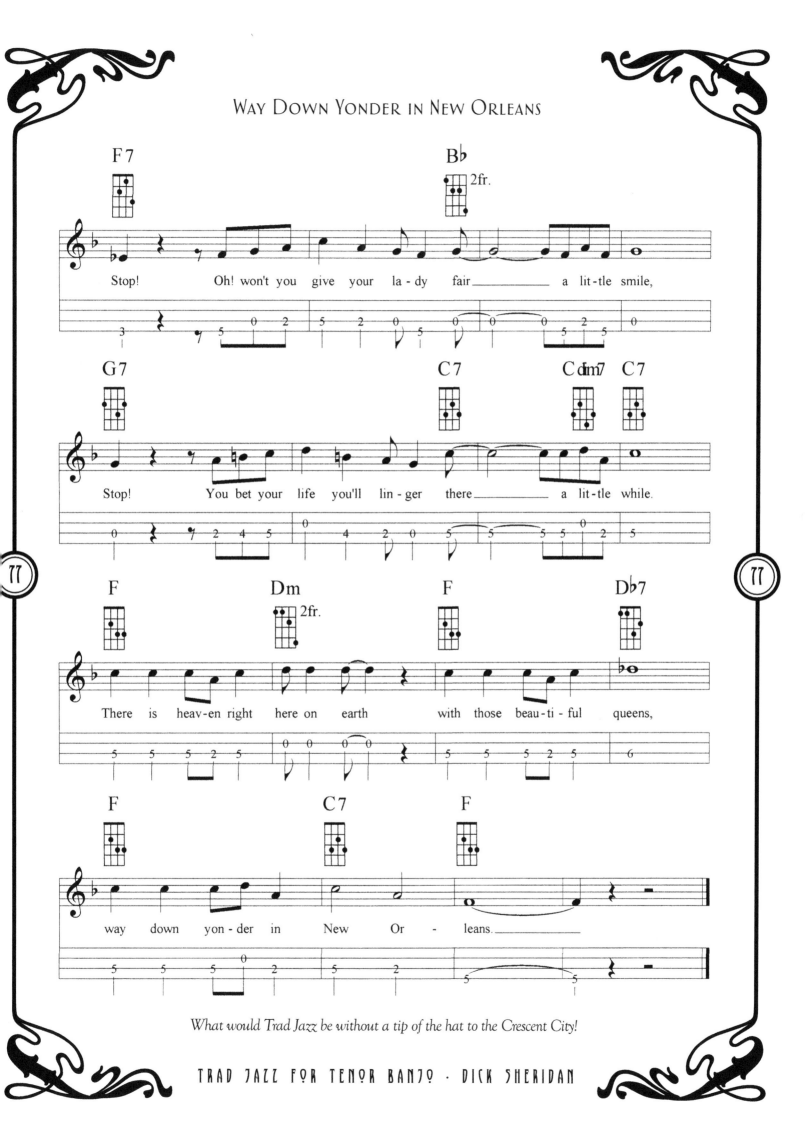

What would Trad Jazz be without a tip of the hat to the Crescent City!

TRAD JAZZ FOR TENOR BANJO · DICK SHERIDAN

WHEN THE SAINTS GO MARCHING IN

Tenor Banjo tuning: CGDA

Traditional

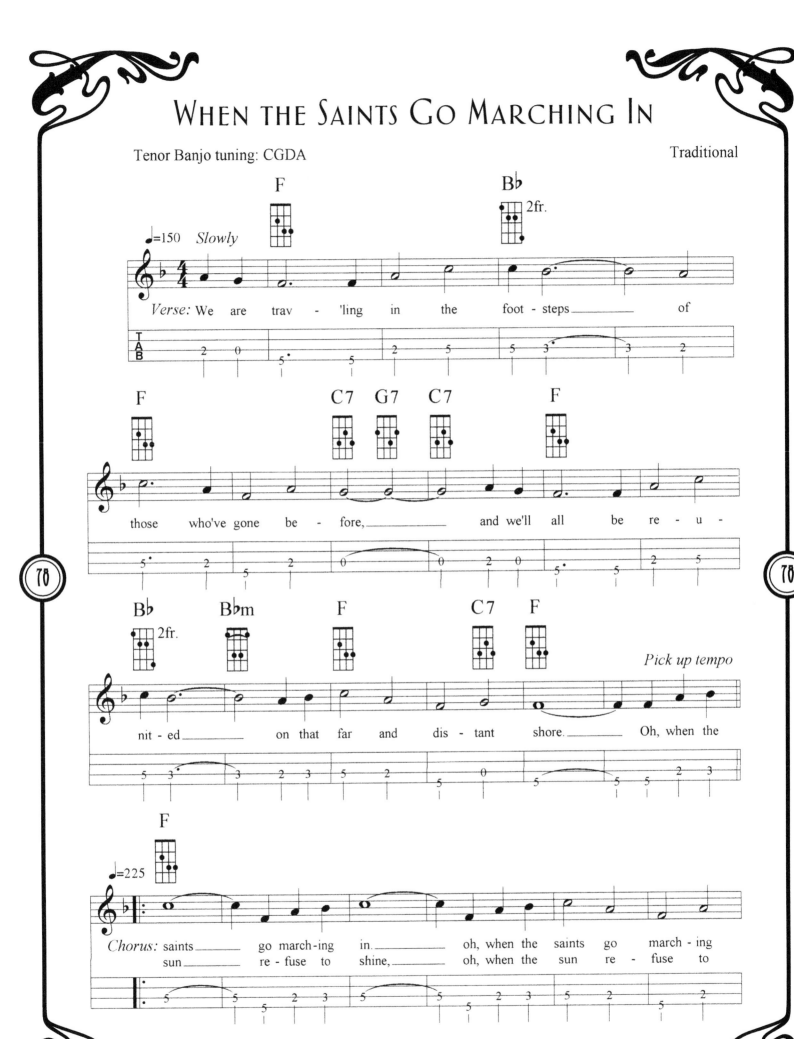

TRAD JAZZ FOR TENOR BANJO · DICK SHERIDAN

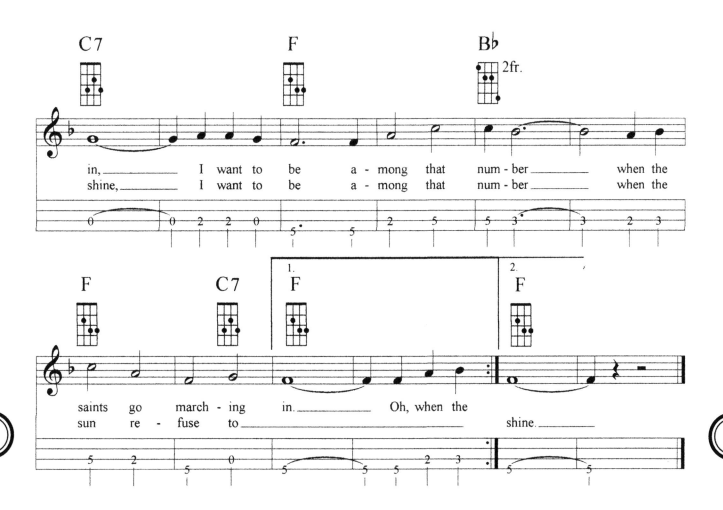

Without a doubt, "Saints" is the song most commonly associated with Dixieland jazz, especially by those whose knowledge of the idiom is pretty much limited to just that one song alone. Bands are requested to play it so often I'm told in *Preservation Hall* - that iconic location of trad jazz in New Orleans - there's a sign on the wall that says:

REQUESTS
$1.⁰⁰
"SAINTS"
$5.⁰⁰

ABOUT THE AUTHOR

Dick Sheridan's introduction to traditional jazz and the tenor banjo came when he was in college in the 1950s. Dixieland (as trad jazz was known then) was going through a major revival from its roots in the early 1900s. It was especially popular on college campuses, and so it was in Dick's college. A band was formed and Dick was recruited to play banjo. He was a ukulele player, not a banjoist, but a mandolin-banjo was found, the number of strings reduced from eight to four, and the instrument was tuned like a ukulele. Soon after, a virtually unused tenor banjo was discovered in an antique shop, and the mandolin-banjo was replaced, although the new banjo was still tuned like a ukulele.

The urge to play an authentic banjo tuning prompted Dick to take a few lessons, and along with the help of self-instruction tutors and chord charts, the conversion was on its way. He could hear the chord progressions, so it was just a matter of replacing uke chords with those for the tenor.

A campus radio station played Dixieland selections every evening, and Dick would run from the dining hall, grab his new banjo, turn on the radio, and try to keep up with the songs he was hearing. Many of the selections that are now considered as standards were then unfamiliar to him, although the chord progressions were somewhat predictable and he could hear the changes. At first it was hard to keep up with the recordings, but in time as the songs and new chord shapes became more familiar ~ and the campus band more active ~ slowly things began to fall into place.

After graduation and military service the banjo was a constant companion, although there was no opportunity for organized band work. But still, the instrument proved perfect for accompanying sing-alongs, jam sessions, and party fun.

Dick recalls a funny experience when he was stationed in Okinawa and had brought his banjo with him. When he first entered his living quarters carrying the banjo in its case, there were a number of house girls who did laundry and domestic work who expressed great interest in what he was carrying. "Kore wa nan desu ka?" they asked, "What is it?" When he said "banjo" they all started to giggle and laugh. Only later he found the Okinawan

Author Dick Sheridan
Circa 1960

(Japanese) word for toilet was "benjo" and he was thought to be carrying a portable potty.

While in Okinawa, the head of Dick's Lyric tenor banjo split wide open. A similar replacement proved impossible since none of the small indigenous music shops had anything resembling either a calfskin or plastic head. The native instrument samisen, however, was somewhat like a banjo since it too had a drum-like head, although it was typically covered with the skin of a snake. Since there was no other alternative, a large snake skin was fitted to the banjo, and that remained in place, scales and all, for over 15 years until it finally wore through. It proved something of a conversation piece and was used to advertise one venue where Dick subsequently played:
~RAGTIME PIANO & SNAKE SKIN BANJO~

Following military service Dick relocated to upstate New York where he initially played with a "happy hour" jazz band at a local military base, then with a newly formed Dixie group that is still in existence some 50 years later. He now leads and plays tenor banjo with this group, as well as playing banjo with various other bands in the area and beyond.

Besides the tenor banjo, Dick plays and privately teaches all the fretted string instruments including guitar, 5-string banjo, ukulele, and mandolin.

More Great Books from Dick Sheridan...

More Great Banjo Books from Centerstream...